THE DENT MASTER MUSICIANS

D0994433

The Dent Master Musicians Series

Titles available in paperback

Titles available in hardback

In preparation

A list of all Dent books on music is obtainable from the publishers:

J. M. Dent Ltd
The Orion Publishing Group
Orion House
5 Upper St Martin's Lane
London WC2H 9EA

THE DENT MASTER MUSICIANS

TCHAIKOVSKY

Edward Garden

J. M. DENT, LONDON

First published 1973
First paperback edition 1976
Reprinted 1978, 1984, 1993

Typeset by Selwood Systems,
Midsomer Norton

Printed and bound in Great Britain
by Butler & Tanner Ltd,
Frome and London

for
J. M. Dent Ltd
The Orion Publishing Group
Orion House
5 Upper St Martin's House
London WC2H 9EA

British Library Cataloguing-in-Publication Data

A catalogue record for this book is available from The British Library

ISBN: 0 460 86110 7

To the Hon. Lady Farrer

Preface

THIS IS not a volume of the complete 'life and works' type. That would be impossible in the limited space at my disposal. Nevertheless it will serve both as an introduction to Tchaikovsky for the general reader and also, I hope, as a long overdue reassessment of a composer whose compositions tend to produce a totally different though equally stereotyped reaction in the sophisticated critic on the one hand, and the plain, unprejudiced listener on the other. It replaces Edwin Evans's volume, the original edition of which dates from as long ago as 1906, since when substantial new Russian material has become available.

The sources used in the book are given in the Select Bibliography (Appendix D). To save space, reference letters have been used in the footnotes. These refer to the appropriate volume in the Bibliography. My thanks are particularly due to Dr Gerald Abraham and Professor Ian Sneddon for lending me their Russian materials.

To avoid confusion I have used the dual system of dates. In each case the first date given is the Russian one, 'old style', and the second is the equivalent according to the Western calendar.

I should like to thank my mother-in-law for her kind encouragement. Much of the book was written in her house, and I have dedicated it to her.

February 1973   Edward Garden

Note on the 1993 reprint

On the occasion of the fourth reprint in 1993, the centenary year of Tchaikovsky's death, the manner of which has caused controversy, current thinking on the matter has been incorporated. Although the book remains substantially unchanged, other emendations have been made. It was first published two decades ago at a time when Tchaikovsky's musical reputation had sunk into a critical slough from which it has now completely emerged. David Brown's substantial tetralogy on Tchaikovsky's life and works has been completed, and details are given in an addendum to the select bibliography. No one now questions that such a massive scholarly examination of Tchaikovsky and his works has been a worthwhile exercise, and the reader is referred to Brown's work for more detailed information than has been possible in this short volume. In addition, the late Galina von Meck, Tchaikovsky's great-niece, translated into English two volumes of letters, including one of correspondence between Tchaikovsky and her grandmother Nadezhda. These are highly recommended, and the reader may also care to dip into Alexandra Orlova's selections from the composer's letters ingeniously interweaved to make a narrative 'self-portrait' of Tchaikovsky. Details of these and other volumes are also to be found in the addendum to the bibliography, but obviously the considerable amount of new material which will no doubt be published on Tchaikovsky in 1993 has not appeared in time to be included.

Sheffield, September 1992   E.G.

Contents

Illustrations

The child, the adolescent and the young man (1840–1866)

On 25 April/7 May 1840 a second son, Peter, was born to the second wife of Ilya Petrovich Tchaikovsky, who, at forty-five, was chief inspector of the Kamsko-Votkinsk mines in the Vyatka government. In this metallurgical centre Ilya was a prominent citizen, a charming but unassuming and only moderately intelligent middle-class government official. Peter's elder brother Nicholas had been born two years earlier, and before two years had elapsed his sister Alexandra (nicknamed Sasha) arrived; later additions to the family were Hippolyte, in 1844, and the twins Anatol and Modest in 1850. (By his previous marriage Ilya had had one daughter, Zinaida.)

Peter's mother was descended from a French Huguenot immigrant family. Her father, André Assier, was a fairly distinguished state councillor, a nervous, impulsive man. There was said to be epilepsy in the family. Peter's French blood has always been made much of by those who seek to explain the alleged fact that his music is more Westernized than that of the Russian 'nationalist' composers, but more important than this very dubious supposition was his unarguably neurotic inheritance from his mother's side of the family, beginning with the morbidly passionate nature of his regard for her with its rather usual corollary of sexual inversion, and progressing towards a propensity for nervous breakdowns unparalleled by any other great composer.

In November 1844 Peter's mother engaged a French governess of Protestant Swiss origin for Nicholas and her niece Lydia, who lived with the family at Votkinsk.[1] Fanny Dürbach was twenty-two years old at this time. At once Peter, never restrained in his emotions, attached himself to her and insisted on sharing the lessons. The four years of her stay were a happy period for the children and especially for Peter. This sensitive, kindly young woman, though not musical and inclined to think that the effect of music upon him was unhealthy,

[1]RN, p. 13.

knew very well how to cope with his emotional tantrums, exceptional even for a child of his age, and with his excessive reaction to criticism – a trait which never deserted him. Fanny provided a more immediate contact than Peter's adored but less emotionally approachable and less understanding mother. Her 'porcelain child' developed swiftly under her, precociously composing (atrociously sentimental) verses in French and starting a life of Joan of Arc[2] which, not surprisingly, proceeded no further than the first chapter. He also learnt German and clearly he had a facility for languages.

Late in 1845 Peter started having piano lessons with one Maria Markovna Palchikova, a freed serf.[3] He was soon able to sight-read as well as she, and later taught himself to play two Chopin mazurkas made known to him not by Palchikova but by a Polish visitor to the family named Maszewski. As early as September 1844 he and Sasha had put together (by ear) a song entitled 'Our Mama in Petersburg', as their proud father wrote to his wife who was on a visit to that city. In addition to a piano, the Tchaikovsky household boasted an 'orchestrion', a large musical-box provided with stops. The cranking of its handle produced arias from *Don Giovanni* and the operas of Rossini, Bellini and Donizetti, which Peter would imitate on the piano. Fanny later recalled that Peter was frequently nervous and unsettled after playing the piano or listening to music.[4] After a musical evening for which he had been allowed to stay up she found him sitting up in bed crying feverishly. When asked what was the matter he replied: 'Oh! this music, this music.' But the house was quiet and there was no music to be heard. 'It's here, here,' he went on by way of explanation, pointing at his head. 'I can't get rid of it. It won't leave me in peace.'

It was nothing short of catastrophic for Peter that he was suddenly jolted out of this happy existence by the decision of his father, now the equivalent of a major-general, to resign from the government service on the naïve assumption, as it turned out, that a suitable post awaited him in Moscow. Fanny Dürbach was dismissed and the family set out for the ancient capital on 26 September/8 October 1848.[5] On their arrival (9/21 October) they discovered that the job for which Ilya had hoped had been snatched by somebody on the spot, and that cholera, a dreaded disease which was eventually to carry off Peter's

[2] *ibid.*, p. 14.
[3] RH, Vol. I, p. 43.
[4] *ibid.*, p. 44.
[5] *ibid.*, p. 45.

mother, was raging. The family hurried on to St Petersburg. During this time the children were in the care of the singularly unlovable and rather bossy Zinaida, since their mother was too preoccupied with the business of travel, settling, resettling and so on to attend to them.

This appalling disruption of a previously cosy existence had a traumatic effect on Peter, and the fact that he and Nicholas were almost immediately sent to the fashionable Schmelling school, where they were teased as country bumpkins and absurdly overworked, did not help matters. Both Nicholas and Peter very soon caught measles in an epidemic at the school, but Nicholas's quick recovery was not matched by his brother, whose continuing malaise was diagnosed by the doctor as 'spinal brain' disease. Six months' complete rest was prescribed. But the boy continued to mope, as his fussing mother with peculiar lack of understanding wrote to Fanny Dürbach (now happily employed with another family): 'He's quite changed, he lazes about, I don't know what to do with him. I often feel like bursting into tears.'[6]

Before the attack of measles he had started piano lessons with a man named Filippov, but as a result of his subsequent state of health these were cut short. He was taken more than once to the opera, but it was only after the appointment of a new governess, Anastasya Petrovna Petrova, at the end of 1849 that his mother was able to write to Fanny Dürbach that Peter was 'becoming more reasonable'. Meanwhile Ilya had found a suitable job as manager of privately owned mines in the distant provincial towns of Alapayevsk and Nizhny-Nevyansk near the Siberian border beyond the Urals, not far from Ekaterinburg. Nicholas was left at school, but the rest of the family moved to Alapayevsk in early June. This meant not only more disorientation for the sadly bewildered child but further neglect of his musical studies, although he wrote to Fanny Dürbach early in 1850: 'I am never away from the piano, which cheers me up when I feel sad.'[7] Already Peter's introversion and self-preoccupation were maturing to the point of egocentricity. And he was already looking back on Fanny's time with the family as a never-to-be-forgotten golden age in his life. This idealization of the past, begun so early in life, was matched only by his idealization of 'woman', first in the form of Fanny Dürbach and his mother, then, as we shall see, in the form of one or two lady loves with whom he studiously avoided anything in the nature of close proximity (with one disastrous exception) and finally

[6]RN, p. 18.
[7]*ibid.*, p. 20.

in the form of heroines in his operas, such as Tatyana in *Eugene Onegin* and Liza in *The Queen of Spades*. Even before puberty the seeds of homosexuality were there, whether or not we agree with Weinstock that his obsessive love of his mother 'had all the intensity of a lover's passion', and that it revealed a 'subconscious desire to leave [the world] by re-entering the womb from which he had issued'.[8] That Peter's later homosexuality may have been congenital is not necessarily supported by the fact that Modest, one of his 'angelic' twin brothers born on May 1/13 – the other was Anatol – was to be a homosexual, as was Sasha's son Vladimir (nicknamed Bob), since according to Dr D.J.West homosexual tendencies might be transmitted by family association.[9] (Dr West does not here mean physical homosexual association, but rather association with a certain type of family upbringing.)

Three months later Peter's mother took him to St Petersburg to the preparatory department of the School of Jurisprudence which he entered as a boarder. Before leaving they went together to a performance of Glinka's *A Life for the Tsar*, which made a lasting impression on him. When the time came for her departure, Peter had a fit of hysterics and had to be separated from her by main force.[10] The dreadful memory of this painful scene remained with him for the rest of his life and invariably caused him to indulge in a shudder of horror. Almost immediately another unfortunate event served to nurture his developing guilt complex. Since his parents lived at such an enormous distance from the capital, his mother had arranged that Modest Alekseyevich Vakar should look after him. When in November there was an epidemic of scarlet fever in the school, Vakar took the boy to live with him until it was over. Peter himself escaped the disease, but on 24 November/6 December his guardian's eldest son died of it. Needless to say Peter blamed himself for this tragedy, though the dead boy's parents tried to impress upon him that he was in no way responsible. Once again he was overcome by depression, but after he had returned to the school he soon settled down to its routine.

The previous autumn Ilya had visited St Petersburg, and father and son enjoyed each other's companionship. But there was no tearful scene on *his* departure. The following year (1852) was very happy. At the end of May/beginning of June his father retired on his savings and

---

[8] EY, p. 29.
[9] D.J.West, *Homosexuality* (London, 1968), p. 161.
[10] RH, Vol. I, p. 61.

state pension and the family moved to St Petersburg. Peter achieved excellent results in the exams for entry to the School of Jurisprudence proper, and the whole family spent a delightful summer holiday on a country estate not far from the capital. His mother's sister, E. A. Alekseyeva, taught him the soprano part in a florid duet from Rossini's *Semiramide* in which she herself sang the contralto. Peter sang 'beautifully and with great aplomb'.[11] His aunt also had a vocal score of *Don Giovanni* which he studied thoroughly.

Both the critic Vladimir Stassov and the composer Serov had been at the School of Jurisprudence, and in their day music had flourished there; but in Tchaikovsky's time the school was more active in the literary field than the musical. One of his class-mates was the future poet Apukhtin. Under a French émigré tutor a hand-copied school magazine was produced, to which Tchaikovsky contributed 'A History of Literature in Our Class'. He passed all his exams without showing exceptional ability. When at the age of nineteen he finally graduated from the establishment his place was thirteenth in his class, which perhaps proves nothing more than that many of his contemporaries were better able to benefit from the kind of teaching employed at the school than he was.

Meanwhile in the summer of 1854 Tchaikovsky's mother died of cholera. Except for a letter written to Fanny Dürbach two and a half years after the event[12] there are unfortunately no extant writings by Tchaikovsky himself about the effect this disaster had upon him. But this mother-worshipping boy of fourteen was certainly cruelly stricken at the time, although it must be pointed out that in the long run it is easier to worship a hallowed memory than an ageing and somewhat corpulent and only rather erratically sympathetic mother-figure composed of mere flesh and blood. The family spent the summer at Oranienbaum on the Gulf of Finland opposite Kronstadt, so that Tchaikovsky's father, who had also succumbed to cholera, could recuperate. Not only did he successfully fight off the disease but he lived on for another twenty-six years and finally died peacefully of old age in his eighty-fifth year (having married for the third time in his seventies). Perhaps it was the infuriating placidity of this easy-going man even in the event of his wife's death which drove his son, miserable to the point of acute melancholia at the intolerable knowledge that he would never see his beloved mother again, to turn to music as an

[11] RH, Vol. I, p. 83.
[12] RI, Vol. V, pp. 56–7.

anodyne. He later declared that his only comfort during this period was music, and it is not in the least surprising that his first definite attempts at composition date from the time of this holiday at Oranienbaum. All his life composition remained for Tchaikovsky an emotional outlet, a substitute for unfulfilled yearnings and unassuaged sexual passion.

In the course of the summer he composed a *Valse dédiée à m-lle Anastasie* (Anastasya Petrova, his former governess) and toyed with the idea of writing an opera called *Hyperbole* to a libretto by V.I. Olkhovsky. Nothing came of this because there were 'too many arias and recitatives and not enough duets and trios'.[13] In the autumn Tchaikovsky had some singing lessons with Gabriel Lomakin, who eight years later was to start the Free School of Music with Balakirev. Up to this time he had been having piano lessons with the music teacher at the school of Jurisprudence, but early in 1855 he was taken on by a much more proficient musician, Rudolf Kündinger, who also recommended that his brother should give him elementary instruction in thorough-bass. A few months later Tchaikovsky's father asked Kündinger whether it would be wise for his son to go in for a musical career. He replied that it would not be advisable, 'in the first place because I saw no signs of genius in Tchaikovsky, and secondly because in my experience the lot of a musician in Russia at that time was an onerous one.'[14]

In 1855 the Tchaikovsky family moved into Ilya's elder brother's house. His sister-in-law was hospitable and relations called Schobert also joined the household. Through these people Tchaikovsky the following year, at the impressionable age of sixteen, met an Italian singing teacher named Luigi Piccioli, a rather odd person who dyed his hair and painted his face in order to simulate a youthful bloom long since vanished. Modest wrote: 'The chief bond between these two friends was music.'[15] Under Piccioli's influence Italian opera became for a time Tchaikovsky's main musical preoccupation. He composed one or two unimportant songs such as 'My genius, my angel, my friend' to words by Fet, but much more to the point was his first printed composition 'Mezza Notte', *Romance pour soprano ou ténor avec accompagnement de piano* (printed, probably at the composer's expense, in 1860) in which the influence of Italian opera is paramount.

[13] *ibid.*, p. 55.
[14] RN, p. 24 *et seq.*
[15] RH, Vol. I, pp. 126–7.

Piccioli particularly liked the operas not only of Rossini but, of more lasting importance, of Bellini, Donizetti and the young Verdi. 'Mezza Notte', despite its importance in revealing the development of the composer's tastes, is otherwise of no interest at all – a piece of entirely derivative empty banality.

After he had left school in 1859, and taken up a post as a first-class clerk in the Ministry of Justice, the good-looking youth became very much the young-man-about-town, foppish to the point of dandification – a perfectly ordinary reaction for a boy suddenly released from the ridiculous regimentation of such a school as he had attended. He took part in amateur plays at the house of a family named Yesipov, played dance music at parties, flirted ostentatiously but distantly with young ladies such as Sophie Herngross, who flattered his vanity by admiring him. He went frequently to the theatre, the ballet and the opera where he greatly enjoyed Weber's *Der Freischütz* and, very significantly, Meyerbeer's *Les Huguenots* in addition to his favourite *Don Giovanni* and *A Life for the Tsar*, not to mention the Verdi and other Italian operas first introduced to him by Piccioli.

On the 10/22 March 1861 he wrote to his sister Sasha, now married to L. V. Davydov and living at Kamenka in the Ukraine, that his father was not entirely opposed to his taking up a musical career and that he was to study thorough-bass.[16] The difficulty was that Ilya had lost all his savings in a rash speculation three years before and, although he had subsequently been able to obtain a job as Director of the Technological Institute, his income was not sufficient for him to be able to give his son an allowance. So Tchaikovsky did not for the time being leave the Ministry of Justice and concentrate on music as he would have liked. His tutor was to be Zaremba, who believed wholeheartedly in the harmonic theories of Adolph Marx and the efficacy of a musical training in strict counterpoint. For Tchaikovsky this was to be the first staging post on the road to a possible musical career. Meanwhile he spent the summer touring Western Europe with a friend of his father's. In Paris he went to *Il Trovatore* and *Les Huguenots*, but compared these performances unfavourably with their Petersburg counterparts, with the exception of the production and the ensemble which were 'remarkably good'.[17]

Zaremba's classes were held in the Mikhailovsky Palace and spon-

[16] RL, p. 4.
[17] RL, p. 9 and RI, Vol. V, pp. 68–9, in a letter to his father dated 12/24 August, 1861. The date is incorrectly given as 12/24 March in RN, p. 30.

sored by the Russian Musical Society. One of the leading lights in the Directorate of the R.M.S. was a widowed German lady, the Grand Duchess Helena Pavlovna. Born the Princess of Saxe-Altenburg, and later to be a fanatical opponent of Balakirev and the 'new Russian school', she persuaded the Emperor to grant a subsidy towards a new Conservatoire of Music, which duly opened under the directorship of Anton Rubinstein in September 1862. Zaremba's classes were transferred there and Tchaikovsky became a student at the Conservatoire in order to continue the course, now increased to two classes a week – one in harmony and one in counterpoint.[18] Because he was still in the employment of the Ministry of Justice he initially restricted himself to these classes, but by the end of 1862 he had also joined the composition class of the Director himself.

His work at the Ministry was becoming more and more of a burden to him. The well-known legend that he once absentmindedly tore off small pieces from an official document while talking to a colleague, rolled them into paper pellets and after due mastication devoured them altogether, does not necessarily imply that, just because in a moment of abstraction this paper was substituted for his more usual diet of concert programmes, he adopted a lackadaisical attitude to his work. Be that as it may, his heart was certainly not in it. The question was, was it wise to give up a safe if boring post and devote himself entirely to music? Whether or not he was good enough to risk such a thing still seemed a debatable point, but after a good deal of dithering he finally took the plunge in the spring of 1863 in a fit of pique at being passed over for promotion at the Ministry. He wrote to his sister: 'I'm at least sure of one thing, that I'll be a good musician at the end of the course.'[19] He had received some words of encouragement from Anton Rubinstein,[20] even if these were only in the form of a rebuke to the effect that one who was 'definitely talented' ought to take his work more seriously.

He was quick to take this advice, and soon became a grubby, hard-working student no less true to type than the discarded young-man-about-town character had been. At the Conservatoire he made friends with Hermann Laroche, a German-Russian boy five years his junior and later a violent advocate on his behalf, though he was equally violently antagonistic to Balakirev's group (which neither he nor

[18] RC, Vol. I, p. 43.
[19] RI, Vol. V, p. 77.
[20] According to Laroche (RC, Vol. I, pp. 40–1) this was Zaremba, but Kashkin insists that it was Rubinstein himself (RB, pp. 7–8).

Tchaikovsky were to meet for a number of years). This wide-eyed youth, crowned by a thick mop of charmingly uncontrollable hair, boosted Tchaikovsky's ego by believing that he would become a great artist, for which Tchaikovsky fervently hoped, even if he had untruthfully averred the contrary in a letter to his sister the previous autumn. His elder brother Nicholas was horrified at the risky step he was taking and stated bluntly that he very much doubted if Tchaikovsky would ever become another Glinka. While agreeing with him in this, he replied that the day would come when 'you'll be proud to be my brother'.[21] He was given the opportunity to act as an accompanist at two concerts, he told his sister in a letter of 15/27 April,[22] and he played at one of Helena Pavlovna's musical evenings. In this letter, as in others, he mentions his twin brothers 'Toly' and 'Modi,' of whom he had become very fond now that the rest of the family were away from home. All the affection of which he was capable was lavished upon them to make up for the fact that they had no mother, as he put it. At this time he started giving piano lessons to eke out his living.

The following month rehearsals started for Alexander Serov's *Judith*, an opera much indebted to Meyerbeer but also containing original features which were to influence Mussorgsky. (The previous year Serov had sung the praises of Wagner when he had visited St Petersburg and conducted in addition to some of his earlier operas excerpts from the completed parts of the *Ring*.) Tchaikovsky attended some of the rehearsals and the first performance on 16/28 May. The opera created a furore which disgusted Vladimir Stassov, the critic whose support was so important to Balakirev and his circle.[23] But unlike Stassov many of the Conservatoire students were numbered with the approving herd, Tchaikovsky among them, and his admiration for the opera hardly diminished in later years. For in his estimation it had passed one of the most important tests: it had been triumphantly successful, as was its successor *Rogneda*. Serov remained until his death in the early seventies one of the most popular native composers in Russia.

Concerts in the 1860s were few and far between, no more than a dozen or so every year in St Petersburg sponsored by the Russian Musical Society, two at the Free School and the odd students' concert at the Conservatoire. On the other hand, there was a full winter season of opera. Most of the great European singers sang in Petersburg at

---

[21] RH, Vol. I, p. 129.
[22] RL, pp. 14–15.
[23] EU, p. 52.

one time or another, and there were sometimes important premières there. For instance, Verdi's *La Forza del Destino* received its first performance at the Maryinsky Theatre late in 1862. Tchaikovsky will certainly have been present on that occasion as he was in the case of Serov's *Judith* the following year, and it may well be that the seeds of the idea of an inescapable 'Fatum' which was gradually to obsess him over the years in his personal life and in his music were sown at this time, not to mention the actual influence Verdi had upon some of his music.

In addition to his classes in composition, instrumentation, counterpoint and harmony (he had been excused the compulsory piano class) Tchaikovsky had some organ lessons and took up the flute so that he could play in the Conservatoire orchestra. Under his own baton this small orchestra played his newly composed Overture in F major. Laroche reported that he conducted with his right hand only and held his left under his chin to prevent his head falling from his shoulders, which in his stage-fright he imagined was an imminent possibility. Other attempts at composition were a String Quartet in B♭ major with, as the main subject of the slow movement, a Ukrainian folk-song which he used also in a *Scherzo à la Russe* for piano, Op. 1 No. 1; an orchestral *Dance of the Serving Maidens*, curiously enough performed at Pavlovsk in the summer of 1865 under the direction of none other than Johann Strauss; a setting of the love scene between Marina and the Pretender from Pushkin's *Boris Godunov*; and as a leaving cantata, the equivalent of a graduation thesis, a setting of Schiller's *An die Freude* for soloists, chorus and orchestra, first performed at the ceremony of the distribution of prizes on 31 December 1865/12 January 1866 in the absence of the composer, who was unable to bring himself to undergo the public viva voce examination at the graduation. Though angry, Rubinstein nevertheless allowed him to receive the coveted diploma. But together with such disparate critics as the pro-nationalist Cui, who wrote a scathing review which wounded Tchaikovsky deeply, and Serov, the 'perfect Wagnerite', and with the exception only of the still insignificant young student Laroche, he roundly condemned the cantata.

Rubinstein's condemnation had been even more pronounced in the case of a previous and much more important composition. Tchaikovsky had been greatly impressed by the well-known dramatist Ostrovsky's *The Storm*. This tragedy had received its first performance in 1860. At that time Tchaikovsky did not know the works of Schumann nor even how many symphonies Beethoven had written. His original project of writing an opera on *The Storm* fell through, but in the summer of

1864 Rubinstein required him to write an overture as a holiday task. During these four years he had made up many of the earlier deficiencies in his musical education and had become acquainted with some of the works not only of Beethoven and Schumann, but of Berlioz, Liszt and Henri Litolff, whose overtures and piano concertos he admired. Rather curiously, he first heard the works of these composers performed by Rubinstein himself, although the latter would not let his pupils use an orchestra larger than would have been approved of by Mendelssohn or Schumann. Tchaikovsky's holiday exercise took the heretical form of a concert overture with a programme based on *The Storm*, scored for a considerably larger orchestra than Rubinstein normally allowed. As well as frowning upon the use of tremolo strings, harp, tam-tam, tuba and cor anglais, all employed in the overture, Rubinstein was still withholding the cachet of his approval from programme music itself.

Tchaikovsky spent the summer of 1864 as a guest of Prince Golitsin at Trostinets in the province of Kharkov. When he had completed his overture he excitedly dispatched it to Laroche,[24] asking him to show it to Rubinstein, who was appropriately outraged by the whole thing. Its form was perfunctory, its orchestration monstrous and its material puerile and crude. Anton's brother Nicholas, later more sympathetic towards Tchaikovsky's music, was also to disapprove of the work. But an examination of the score shows that the Rubinsteins were quite wrong totally to condemn this admittedly somewhat naïve work.

At the twenty-third bar of the introductory *Andante misterioso* Tchaikovsky employs the Russian folk-song 'Iskhodila Mladenka' (later to be used by Mussorgsky in *Khovanshchina*), which he scores beautifully for cellos and cor anglais. It was perhaps not entirely fortuitous that Balakirev's *Second Overture on Russian Themes* had received its first performance in St Petersburg only a few months previously. Among the many histrionic devices that trace their origins from Meyerbeer and French grand opera are timpani rolls punctuated by *fortissimo tutti* chords, a passage for *pianissimo* trombones to the periodic accompaniment of strokes of the tam-tam, passages for trombones in octaves accompanied by disjointed skirls on the strings, the use of low wind chords and muted trumpet (just before the recapitulation of the main *Allegro vivo* theme), passages emphasizing each strong beat with an uninhibited clash of the cymbals, or the use

24RC, Vol. I, p. 47.

of *fortissimo* chords off the beat, and so on.[25] Operatic in origin, too, is the distinctly Verdian main subject of the *Allegro vivo*, which is, however, developed much in the repetitious Lisztian 'wall-paper pattern' manner, with a dash of Litolff thrown in. Still more attributable to Liszt is the fugal passage in the 'development' section, the opening of which is (probably unconsciously) a straight crib from the first subject of Liszt's E♭ major Piano Concerto. Tchaikovsky disclaimed much knowledge of Liszt at this time, too modestly it seems. The second subject, a sweeping love-theme, is a beautiful melody of the 'Bellini-with-a-Russian-accent' type, as Gerald Abraham has described the species of which Tchaikovsky was the supreme master. It has here, in the second part of its first main phrase, more than a touch of Balakirev too. It would not look out of place in many of Tchaikovsky's more mature compositions.

Many of the fingerprints of Tchaikovsky's future musical style, then, are evident in this score; traces of Bellini, Verdi, Meyerbeer, Liszt, Litolff, Balakirev and Russian folk-music; and in spite of its manifest weaknesses it deserved more from the Rubinstein brothers than a pronouncement that a performance was 'quite impossible'.[26]

[25] These effects were introduced by Meyerbeer 'pour épater le bourgeois', as Théophile Gautier put it.
[26] RH, Vol. I, p. 171.

2

Early years in Moscow (1866–9)

Nicholas, Anton Rubinstein's brother, had founded the Moscow branch of the Russian Music Society in 1860, and four years later he moved to a larger house in which he and several colleagues taught various musical subjects. This establishment was granted an Imperial Charter, but was initially much humbler than its sister Conservatoire in the northern capital. In 1865 he invited Serov to become professor of harmony, but that much-lauded composer was loath to bury himself in provincial Moscow, especially as the salary which Nicholas was able to offer him was now hardly tempting to one in his position. In any case the plaudits of St Petersburg society and the patronage of the Grand Duchess Helena Pavlovna were not long in ensuring for him a state pension.

Anton Rubinstein suggested to his brother that the young Tchaikovsky should be appointed to the post and, though the salary was very small, he gladly accepted. Soon after his graduation he left Petersburg for Moscow[1] where Nicholas Rubinstein established him in a room in his house, and not only fed him well but fitted him out with presentable clothes. Rubinstein also took him to the opera and to concerts and introduced him to his fellow teachers, but the fledgling professor was very homesick all the same. He particularly missed his twin brothers, writing to them and other members of his family ten letters within his first month or so in Moscow in spite of a very full programme of theatre and concert going, teaching and the time-consuming business of eating and drinking with the rather exaggeratedly convivial Rubinstein, both at home and at the fashionable English Club. In addition he worked on the orchestration of a very uneven Overture in C minor, roughed out the previous summer, which Rubinstein understandably refused to play, though he did perform with some success a newly completed full orchestral version of the

[1]RH, Vol. I, p. 220 *et seq.*

more conventional Overture in F major at a Russian Music Society concert, much to the composer's delight.

These letters[2] tell of Tchaikovsky's homesickness and of his horror at the possibility of having to live in Moscow 'for years – perhaps for ever'; of Rubinstein's 'looking after me as if he were my nurse'; of his introduction to Kashkin, Albrecht and others; of visits to the Tarnovsky family which included 'two delectable nieces', with one of whom he almost persuaded himself he was a little in love,[3] producing some rather heavy-handed 'teasing' on the part of Rubinstein; of his laughing at *Pickwick* (in a Russian translation); of his first lecture at which he was 'terribly ill at ease', although he 'got through it all right' – but a week or two later: 'I'm no longer at all nervous and am slowly managing to adopt a suitably professional air.'

The most distinguished of Tchaikovsky's colleagues was Nicholas Rubinstein, who combined excellent qualities as a pianist and conductor with a flair for organization and a typically aristocratic weakness for women and gambling, together with the very Russian ability to consume an inordinate amount of alcohol. He was consequently not really suitable to be the mentor of a person so easily influenced as Tchaikovsky,[4] who later indulged in occasional bouts of heavy drinking, more often than not in secret, though he never became compulsively addicted to drink. Easy women were not of course for the younger man, nor was he to gamble, except possibly with life itself or 'fate', as he would no doubt have put it. However, as a musical mentor Nicholas was to be preferred to his brother Anton. He was much more in sympathy with the 'new Russian school' as it was called, and was the first to perform many of Tchaikovsky's early compositions.

Other colleagues with whom Tchaikovsky soon became friendly were the music publisher P. I. Jurgenson, the pianist and critic N. D. Kashkin and the cellist Karl Albrecht. Albrecht admired particularly the music of Wagner, Liszt and Schumann. Of these, Tchaikovsky was antipathetic only to Wagner. Liszt's music had already been strongly influential in the *Storm* and C minor overtures, and the influence of Schumann had been marked in the Piano Sonata in C$\sharp$ minor written a few months previously in St Petersburg. This work is so indebted to Schumann in the layout for the hands, the four-square structure, the decoration, the harmonic chromaticism and the charming delicacy, as

---

[2] RI, Vol. V, pp. 90–102.
[3] 'Mufka', as the young lady was intimately called, soon married an army officer.
[4] Tchaikovsky was in fact only five years younger than Rubinstein.

well as the inherent nature of the thematic material, that it is clear that the composer had been closely studying Schumann's piano music, not least the sonatas. It is consequently curious that this is nevertheless the most successful prentice work of Tchaikovsky's, revealing every now and then touches of originality in a medium which was never greatly to inspire him in his maturity.

A year or two later Laroche was appointed to the staff of the Conservatoire, and this may well have exercised a steadying influence on his intimate friend who, encouraged by Rubinstein, had been 'coming home a trifle drunk', 'spending two consecutive evenings at the English Club' and so on, as he wrote to Anatol and Modest. Another member of his immediate circle was N. A. Hubert, also a former fellow student, who Tchaikovsky thought lacked 'character'.[5]

Tchaikovsky's small circle of friends at the Conservatoire, by their constant encouragement and assistance, their performances and criticism of his compositions and, most of all, their genuine friendship, were of vital importance to him both in establishing his reputation as a composer and later in providing some sort of exception to the necessary loneliness which was the lot in those days of the homosexual, unable as he was to establish a firm, constant and loving relationship with any other human being.

Not that Tchaikovsky in the summer of 1866 knew, consciously at any rate, that his homosexual leanings were irreversible. In fact it is possible that the family, hoping that his affection for Vera Davydova, his sister Sasha's sister-in-law, would blossom into something more, gave the poor state of the roads as an excuse for cancelling his holiday with Sasha at Kamenka in the Ukraine and sending him off with Modest to spend a holiday with Vera, her sister Elizabeth and her mother near Peterhof, not far from St Petersburg. This seems all the more likely in that Anatol was quite able to go from St Petersburg to Kamenka as originally planned. It was probably as a result of being unable to feel sexually aroused, of intolerable emotional frustration, that he dispelled all pleasure by taking up again the composition of his First Symphony, started the previous March.[6] It had caused him much difficulty then, but the nervous disorders were terrifyingly increased during the summer when, suffering from insomnia, he worked away at it night and day until the inevitable nervous breakdown brought him to the verge of insanity.[7]

[5]RK, Vol. I, pp. 172–3.
[6]RH, Vol. I, p. 272.
[7]*ibid.*, p. 248.

The following summer he determined to holiday in Finland with Modest, and they got as far as Viborg before they realized that £10 or so was hardly enough to last them for the summer. On their return to Petersburg they found that their father (and with him all hope of a loan) had gone to the Urals. They spent their last coppers on the steamer tickets to Hapsal in Estonia, where they joined the Davydova ladies. Tchaikovsky composed there a set of three piano pieces entitled *Souvenir de Hapsal*, Op. 2, one of which is the well-known *Chant sans paroles*, whose title betrays its provenance, and the others a commonplace Scherzo and an empty romantic salon piece, *Ruines d'un Château*. The pieces are dedicated to Vera, but there are no signs of emotional frustration or even of emotional involvement here. All the same, he still felt that he had to excuse himself to Sasha for not taking things any further with Vera, who fancied herself in love with him. 'Possibly I'm blind and stupid,' he wrote, 'but I swear to you that my regard for her goes no further than ordinary simple friendship.'[8] Besides, he averred he was too lazy to marry.

Next year, however, he did meet someone with whom he believed he was in love. The principal soprano of a visiting Italian opera company, Désirée Artôt, a pupil of Pauline Viardot-Garcia, was a superb artist with a large vocal range and enormous personal charm, though according to Laroche she was not particularly good-looking. She was the star of an otherwise third-rate company. Moscow flocked to hear her. Tchaikovsky's attention to her began to be noticed. Prince Odoyevsky wrote in his diary that the young composer 'courted her a great deal.'[9] On 25 September/7 October 1868,[10] Tchaikovsky wrote: 'Artôt is a wonderful person. We're good friends'; on 21 October/2 November: 'I'm very busy at the moment; I'm writing recitatives and choruses for Auber's *Domino noir*, which have to be done for Artôt's benefit performance'; and, some time in November: 'Ah! Modinka ... if you only knew what a singer and artist Artôt is! ... I'm sorry you can't hear and see her. How enraptured you'd be by her gestures and the grace of her movements and posture!' He dedicated a rather vacuous 'Romance' (Op. 5) for piano to her, but while this hardly proved his passion for her, he wrote again to Modest in December: 'I haven't written to you for a long time, but a variety of circumstances

[8] RI, Vol. V, p. 120.
[9] RN, p. 56.
[10] This and the ensuing letters to Anatol and Modest are to be found in RI, Vol. V, pp. 143–8.

have combined to prevent me from writing letters, for I've devoted all my spare time to a person of whom I rather think you've heard, and of whom I'm very fond.'

On 26 December 1868/7 January 1869 he asked his father for advice:

> As I expect that rumours have reached you of my engagement and you may be annoyed that I've not written to you on the subject, I'll explain what it's all about without more ado. I first became acquainted with Artôt last spring, but saw her only once at a supper party after her benefit performance. After her return here in the autumn a month had elapsed without my calling on her once. Then we happened to meet at a musical evening; she expressed surprise that I hadn't visited her.

It seems, therefore, that the lady took the initiative.

> I promised to call on her [Tchaikovsky continues] but I wouldn't have kept the promise (as I find it difficult to get to know people) if Anton Rubinstein, who happened to be passing through Moscow, had not dragged me to her house. From then on I began to receive almost daily invitations from her and gradually I became accustomed to visiting her every evening.

Prima donnas like to have handsome young men about them, but Tchaikovsky took the flirtation seriously. 'Soon we became inflamed with feelings of great affection for one another, resulting at once in a mutual understanding. It goes without saying that there arose immediately the question of marriage, which we both desire and which ought to be accomplished in the summer if nothing happens to prevent it.' But Tchaikovsky had his mental reservations as well as Artôt. The obstacles in the path leading to wedded bliss included not only his prospective mother-in-law, who considered him too young (he was five years junior to Artôt), and viewed with concern her daughter's probable removal to live in Russia, but Nicholas Rubinstein and other friends, who were

> doing everything in their power to prevent the marriage. They say that in marrying a well-known singer I shall be playing the sorry role of being my wife's husband, that is to say I shall trail along behind her all over Europe, live at her expense and find work quite impossible, in a word that when my ardour has cooled off somewhat, my self-respect will be lost in disillusionment and despair.

This could be avoided if she were to settle down to a domestic life with him in Russia, but 'in spite of all her love' for him, 'she cannot bring herself to give up the stage to which she has got accustomed and which furnishes her with both fame and money'. Tchaikovsky for his part did not want to sacrifice his future. He loved her with all his heart and soul, and felt that 'it is not possible to live any longer without her'. On the other hand 'cool commonsense bids me hesitate ... I am waiting, dear father, for you to write me your views on the matter'.[11]

But, as might have been expected, Tchaikovsky's father left all the decision-making entirely to his son.[12] Not that firm advice to marry or not to marry would have been of any use, since Artôt soon took up with a Spanish baritone named Mariano Padilla y Ramos, if she was not already betrothed to him, and married him a few months later. As a matter of fact Tchaikovsky's desire for her, such as it was, cooled off rather more quickly than it should have done had he been smitten with her to the extent alleged in his letters. Only a week or two later, in a letter to Anatol mainly consisting of news of his musical activities, he inserts: 'As for the love interlude ... I tell you that it's very doubtful whether I shall enter Hymen's kingdom; things are not really going according to plan.'[13]

When he received news of Artôt's marriage from none other than an uninhibitedly gleeful Nicholas Rubinstein, he was hardly heartbroken, though his pride was temporarily wounded. He may genuinely have thought that, all other things being equal, his feelings for Désirée Artôt were strong enough to enable him to achieve a satisfactory sexual relationship with her. After all, homosexuals have found it possible to have heterosexual relationships. But whether or not it would have been possible, it was certainly his last chance. What might have been when he was twenty-eight was to prove impossible at the age of thirty-seven, by which time he had been indulging his homosexual fantasies (if nothing more) to the full, so that his eventual marriage at that age was a traumatic experience.

Just as his infatuation with Désirée Artôt was nothing much more than puppy-love, so Tchaikovsky in these years was only a stage or so beyond the musical puberty reached in the *Storm* overture, though in the late sixties he was suddenly to mature very quickly and, with Balakirev's guidance, to compose his first masterpiece. Not that the earliest compositions lacked very considerable signs of talent and imagination. The most important orchestral example is the First Symphony in G minor, Op. 13. It was begun, as we have seen, in

[11] *ibid.*, pp. 149–50.
[12] RH, Vol. I, pp. 305–8.
[13] RI, Vol. V, p. 153.

March 1866 only a month or two after his arrival in Moscow and, in spite of the nervous collapse brought about by overwork on it at the end of July, it was more or less completed and the orchestration was well enough in hand to show to Anton Rubinstein and Zaremba in St Petersburg in the middle of August. They rejected the symphony, refused to put it down for performance at a Music Society concert the following season and gave him detailed instructions about how it should be altered, but he had to postpone this work for the time being. On 1/13 September the Moscow Conservatoire opened in a new and larger building. Tchaikovsky attended the celebratory banquet at which he overcame his shyness and proposed one of the toasts; after the banquet he played on the piano Glinka's *Russlan and Ludmilla* overture from memory since, according to Kashkin, he was determined that 'Glinka's should be the first music to be heard in the new Conservatoire.'[14] Soon afterwards he set to work on and quickly completed a *Festival Overture on the Danish National Anthem*, which Nicholas Rubinstein commissioned from him to be performed as part of the Moscow celebrations of the Tsarevich's marriage to the Danish princess, Dagmar. (Tchaikovsky immediately sold to his colleague, the pianist A. I. Dubuque, the gold and turquoise cuff-links which the Tsarevich graciously presented him with afterwards.)[15]

At the end of November he had finished revising the symphony and submitted it again to Anton Rubinstein and Zaremba, who were still dissatisfied with it, though the *Adagio* and *Scherzo* were pronounced fit and were duly performed in St Petersburg on 11/23 February 1867. Meanwhile, early in the previous December, Nicholas Rubinstein had performed the *Scherzo* only in Moscow, but it received scant applause; at last, after further alterations, he performed the complete work on 3/15 February 1868 with great success. Tchaikovsky wrote to Anatol that the *Adagio* had been particularly admired.[16]

The symphony opens in a decidedly Mendelssohnian atmosphere similar to the opening of the *Hebrides* overture, and as in the *Italian* Symphony we are plunged straight into the first subject without preamble. The programmatic titles, *Winter Reveries* for the symphony as a whole, *Reveries of a Winter Journey* for the first movement and *Land of Desolation, Land of Mists* for the second, are also derived from Mendelssohn, since they are incidental and have no effect whatever on

[14] N. Kashkin: *Pervoe 25-letiye Moskovskoi Konservatory* (Moscow, 1891), pp. 11–12.
[15] RH, Vol. I, p. 260.
[16] RL, p. 39.

the structure, which in the first movement is 'by' Mendelssohn 'out of' Schumann. While some of the more delicate touches are distinctly Mendelssohnian, which Tchaikovsky knew would please the Rubinsteins, much of the actual layout is Schumannesque.

The surroundings of the first subject may be Mendelssohnian, but the theme itself is of a Russian folk-like nature, turning in upon itself repetitively and reiterating intervals of the third and fourth. It has an important corollary which is not derived from Russian folk-song, Mendelssohn or Schumann, but from opera. One almost expects, after the following example, someone to creep onto the stage and sing, in a hushed whisper, '*mezza notte*'.

Ex. 1

This is modelled not so much on Meyerbeer, though the conspirators plotting the massacre of St Bartholomew in *Les Huguenots* do sing the words 'à min-uit' to the rhythm , as on the Verdi of *Un Ballo in Maschera*. Except for this passage there is nothing operatic about the symphony as a whole. The achievement of climax by means of ascending (or descending) chromatic scales, the full brass climactic version of the themes accompanied by string tremolos and so on are less robustly Meyerbeerian than in the *Storm* and C minor overtures, and much more in the sparer style of the Schumann of the First and Fourth Symphonies (which, together with Mendelssohn's *Italian* Symphony, we know Tchaikovsky played over as duets with the Davydova ladies in the summer of 1866) and, even more importantly, in the style of the dramatic *Manfred* overture, first performed only fourteen years previously. Also indebted to this overture are many of the chromatic devices employed by Tchaikovsky here, for example the harmonization of the first subject which occurs over a more or less chromatically descending scale some twenty bars before the second subject in the exposition.[17] This is comparable to the chromatically descending nature and surroundings of the second subject of the overture. The beautiful second subject of the symphony and its chromatic accompaniment[18] are also Schumannesque, but still more so are many of the techniques used in extension and development such as dotted-note rhythms and tremolo strings,[19] and also typical syncopations.[20] No less derivative from Schumann are the opening and closing bars of the slow movement, and the *Scherzo* with its cross-rhythm of three-eight and three-four. This delightful *Scherzo* is a version of the *Scherzo* from the C$\sharp$ minor Piano Sonata scored for a Mendelssohnian orchestra.

The folk-song element is not confined to the first movement. The main theme of the slow movement is a folk-like melody which at its fifth bar (fig. (i) of Ex. 2a) strongly resembles the 'Song of the Volga Hauliers':

Ex. 2

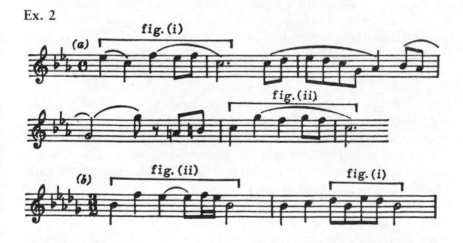

Tchaikovsky included in the first act of an opera he was already contemplating on Ostrovsky's *The Voyevoda* a very similar melody, which he later transferred to *The Oprichnik* (Ex. 2(b)). This kind of

[17] Eulenburg miniature score, p. 10.
[18] E.M.S., pp. 11 and 13.
[19] e.g. E.M.S., pp. 14 and 15.
[20] e.g. E.M.S., p. 19.

melody was to remain deeply embedded in his subconscious mind. For instance, it occurs with little alteration in Act IV of *Swan Lake*.

As if this were not enough, an actual folk-song, 'The gardens bloomed', is employed in the finale of the symphony, first in the slow introduction and then as the second subject of the *Allegro maestoso*, where its treatment at times verges on the banal. The *Scherzo* and trio is the only movement not to employ folk-like materials prominently, and only in the finale is their treatment less than adequate.

The other two important Russian symphonies of the 1860s were Rimsky-Korsakov's First, in E♭ minor,[21] and Borodin's First, in E♭ major. The latter had been largely written by this time but was not publicly performed until early in 1869; the former was first performed by Balakirev in St Petersburg a few weeks before Tchaikovsky's departure for Moscow and hailed by the Petersburg 'new Russian school' as the first Russian symphony (since for them Anton Rubinstein was not 'Russian').

Tchaikovsky was present at the première of Rimsky-Korsakov's symphony, though he did not get to know Borodin's for the next year or two. Hence any similarities between Borodin's work and his own must certainly be ascribed to similar influences and derivations, such as Schumann's *Manfred* overture (in E♭ major/minor), which as a matter of fact Borodin's resembles to a greater extent than does Tchaikovsky's – not least in the cross-rhythms, the chromaticism and particularly in the slow (E♭ minor) introduction, in which the germs of the thematic material of the sonata-form movement are to be found. But whereas Tchaikovsky's *Scherzo* (originally for piano) would not look out of place in Schumann's G minor Piano Sonata, Borodin's is an original *tour de force*, in which it is possible to trace only a fairly distant ancestry in Beethoven and Mendelssohn. Rimsky's *Scherzo* is also charming as well as naïve. All three symphonies have finales rooted in the techniques of Schumann.

But even more important than considering these and other obvious similarities in the musical influences at work on these young composers is the comparison of their use of folk-like materials. The Petersburg group under Balakirev did not yet know Tchaikovsky and were still suspicious of this product of the despised Conservatoire. But it is impossible to agree with Martin Cooper that 'of actual folk-songs Tchaikovsky did not make so much use as the "Mighty Handful" '[22]

---

[21] Later revised and transposed into E minor.
[22] ER (2), p. 35.

(the nickname for Balakirev's group). A great deal of Tchaikovsky's early music is full of actual folk-songs as well as of folk-like materials, mostly very sensitively and judiciously employed. The other two symphonies are influenced much less centrally by folk-song than Tchaikovsky's. There is nothing resembling a folk-song in the first or last movements of Borodin's, composed, as was Rimsky-Korsakov's, under Balakirev's strict surveillance. Only in the exotically 'oriental' slow movement and the superb trio is there anything at all folk-like. This for Balakirev was sufficient. He did not think that a folk-song or its equivalent was suitable to be a main subject in a sonata-form movement, and that a symphony should be merely a hotch-potch of folk melodies. Tchaikovsky's achievement here is to incorporate his theme as a main subject in the structure of his first movement with conspicuous lack of *grotesquerie*. In point of fact, when this movement was played over to Balakirev and his circle by the composer at his first meeting with the whole group in Petersburg in the spring of 1868, Rimsky-Korsakov wrote that it 'pleased us very much. Our former opinion of him gave way to a more favourable one.'[23] There can be no doubt that this child of the Conservatoire was as caught up in the general feeling of emancipation and nationalism of the sixties as were his self-educated contemporaries; and in symphonic terms even at this early stage he proved himself to be the superior of Rimsky-Korsakov if not the equal of Borodin, who in any case was seven years older and correspondingly more mature.

Tchaikovsky was the first of the Russians who are remembered today of the younger generation – as opposed to Glinka, Dargomyzhsky and Serov – to write a folk-opera and to have it produced. His opera was based on *The Voyevoda* by Ostrovsky, author of *The Storm*. Indeed the music of the Introduction to Act II is taken from the opening of the *Storm* overture. (It was also used to open the Overture in C minor; Tchaikovsky was not in the habit of wasting good material.) Tchaikovsky met Ostrovsky soon after his arrival in Moscow and by November of the same year he was writing to Anatol that there was hope that 'Ostrovsky himself will write me a libretto on *The Voyevoda*'.[24]

Soon the composer received the first act from Ostrovsky, started work on it but through a stroke of ill fortune lost it. The busy Ostrovsky did manage to reconstruct it from memory and also sent

[23] RD, p. 69.
[24] RL, p. 33, letter of 8/20 November 1866.

him the first scene of Act II, and the words of Marya's song in the next scene – the music of which was a folk-song noted down by Tchaikovsky himself near Moscow. He also gave the composer the music as well as the words of the folk-song 'Na more utushka' which is used in the opening chorus with one change only – the elimination by Tchaikovsky of a sharp leading-note with which Ostrovsky had sought to 'beautify it' as he wrote ten years later to Rimsky-Korsakov.[25] As a matter of fact Tchaikovsky's views on folk-songs were not nearly so much influenced by the Conservatoire as is generally supposed. Soon after they met in 1876, Leo Tolstoy sent him some folk-songs to arrange; for Tchaikovsky's arrangement, of a folk-song that the composer had noted down himself at Kamenka, in the famous *Andante cantabile* of his first String Quartet had moved Tolstoy to tears. Tchaikovsky thanked him for them, but stated firmly that in the version sent to him most of the songs had been forced into D major, unsuitable for true Russian folk-song, which nearly always has an 'indefinite tonality' more like the ancient church modes. Before they could be adequately set there would have to be an exact transcription of the original songs 'as sung by the people'.

Since no more was forthcoming from Ostrovsky, Tchaikovsky had to write the rest of the libretto himself. He was not really successful, eventually deciding to compress his own third and fourth acts into Act III, and cutting out some of the most dramatically suitable material in the process. By the summer of 1868 the finishing touches had been put to the opera while he was on a visit to Paris. There he was in company with his pupil and beloved friend, the consumptive and wealthy Vladimir Shilovsky, who was in Paris with his guardian Vladimir Begichev (Intendant of the Imperial Theatres in Moscow) in order to consult a specialist.

Rehearsals were started in Moscow in the autumn, but were interrupted by the arrival of Désirée Artôt's company, and the first performance did not take place until 30 January/11 February 1869. It had a 'brilliant success' with the public, Tchaikovsky told Modest.[26] The critics were not so enthusiastic, but less understandable was Laroche's cool critique in *Sovremennaya Letopis*, in which he made the extraordinary statement that in spite of the use of folk-songs it was 'completely lacking in any Russian quality' and revealed 'the absence of any Russian national element'.[27]

[25]RI, Vol. VI, p. 67.
[26]RL, p. 49; RH, Vol. I, p. 313.
[27]RN, p. 59.

No other score of Tchaikovsky's is impregnated through and through with the folk idiom to a greater extent than this. But there is little characterization, and he soon realized that as it stood it would not do. In the late seventies he wrote to Mme von Meck: 'A few of my early things have been preserved, most of them I burned. Among these, *The Voyevoda* (from which the dances were saved) and *Undina* ...'[28] And elsewhere: 'In my *Voyevoda* I was concerned mainly with filigree work and quite forgot the stage and all its conditions.'[29]

He was less than honest with Mme von Meck. Not only the dances but most of the best things in *The Voyevoda* – and very fine they are – were later transferred bodily with very nearly the same instrumentation to *The Oprichnik* (1872), and some of the numbers were used in *Swan Lake* (1876). What is more, *The Voyevoda* may not yet have been consigned to the flames at the time of his letter to Mme von Meck, since he soon after used another melody from it as the second subject of the *Allegro* of the *1812* Overture.[30]

Tchaikovsky made two other abortive attempts at operas before *The Oprichnik*. The libretto of the first of these, *Undina*, was a translation by Count F. A. Sollogub of a libretto by Vernoy de Saint-Georges based on La Motte Fouqué's *Ondine*. He started work on this early in 1869 and had completed and orchestrated the whole thing by July. After a great deal of procrastination the opera committee of the Imperial Theatres in Petersburg to whom it had been submitted rejected it, as it rejected Mussorgsky's original version of *Boris* soon afterwards. As with *The Voyevoda*, Tchaikovsky was to make good use of the best music in it. The bridal procession from Act III became the slow movement of the Second Symphony (1872), and one of the love duets was transferred to *Swan Lake* as Odette's *adagio*. The introduction was used unchanged and Undina's song adapted as Lel's first song in his incidental music to Ostrovsky's *Snow Maiden*.

More of the music was turned to account in his next opera, also on a fantastic subject, S. A. Rachinsky's *Mandragora*, and the only new music he composed for this was a 'chorus of flowers and insects' written late in 1869. This was performed separately under the title 'Chorus of Elves', first by Nicholas Rubinstein in Moscow a year afterwards, and then at a Free School concert in Petersburg by

---

[28] RI, Vol. VIII, p. 435.
[29] *ibid.*, p. 445.
[30] For an exhaustive list of all the borrowings from *The Voyevoda* in *The Oprichnik* and other works, see EO(2), pp. 123–5.

Balakirev, who not surprisingly thought highly of it, since it is permeated with the atmosphere of his favourite opera, Glinka's *Russlan* – and not only the choral Ballet of the Flowers from that opera but the Persian chorus with its hauntingly simple song sung by girls. Tchaikovsky's beautiful and equally simple similarly moulded song is for a chorus of boys with full mixed-choral and orchestral accompaniment, and, like the Persian chorus, introduces characteristic triplets later. But it is the simplicity, delicacy and charm at which Tchaikovsky has aimed here; there is nothing Persian about his chorus, though he does use some exotic harmonies such as the chromatically decorated 'dominant' seventh or 'German' sixth on the flattened sixth of the scale in a tonic context – first used by Meyerbeer in *Le Prophète* and Liszt in the revised version of his Second Piano Concerto, but taken to their hearts and exploited to the full by the Russians. (It has been aptly called the 'Russian sixth' by Gerald Abraham.)

In connection with a visit to Moscow by Berlioz, whom Balakirev had invited to Russia during his first season as conductor of the Russian Musical Society, both Stassov and Balakirev himself were in Moscow and met Tchaikovsky for the first time at the beginning of 1868. The dances from the as yet unfinished *Voyevoda* had been performed by Nicholas Rubinstein the previous month. Balakirev must have heard favourable comments on them while he was in Moscow, for he asked Tchaikovsky to send him the score. Meanwhile Tchaikovsky made his first public appearance as a conductor, directing the dances at a charity concert. At this same concert Rimsky-Korsakov's *Serbian Fantasia* was played, and a critic in *The Entr'acte* who signed himself 'Stranger' praised Tchaikovsky's dances but dismissed Rimsky-Korsakov's piece as 'colourless and lifeless'. Tchaikovsky, who had liked the *Fantasia*, delighted the Petersburg group of composers by publishing a strong criticism of 'Stranger' in *Sovremennaya Letopis*, referring in warm terms both to the *Fantasia* and to Rimsky-Korsakov's symphony.[31] It is not surprising, in consequence, that on his visit to Petersburg in the spring, when he met the whole group, he was given a warm welcome.

Balakirev was not able to perform the *Voyevoda* dances himself so late in the season, but he did give the first Petersburg performance of a newly composed symphonic-fantasia *Fatum* on 17/29 March 1869. Performed three weeks earlier in Moscow by Nicholas Rubinstein, it was dedicated to Balakirev, who none the less had grave doubts about

[31] RN, p. 54; RH, Vol. I, p. 288.

it. He wrote to Tchaikovsky a very characteristic letter in which he maintained that *Fatum* was hastily written, not well thought out and creaked at the joints. He compared it in form with Liszt's *Les Préludes*, which was the nearest work to *Fatum* in form that he could think of. But in that work one thing follows naturally on another. He also advised Tchaikovsky to compare it with Glinka's *Night in Madrid* for masterly fusing together of sections.[32]

Tchaikovsky was not used to the Balakirev treatment and it took him upwards of a month before he could bring himself to answer, a week or so after Balakirev had been forced by the Grand Duchess Helena Pavlovna to resign as conductor of the R.M.S. He expressed his indignation at the treatment Balakirev had received. As to *Fatum*, he had hoped for something in the way of praise, instead of nothing but fault-finding. But he admitted the justice of all Balakirev's remarks.[33]

Tchaikovsky expressed publicly as well as privately his indignation at Balakirev's treatment in a strongly worded article.[34] Balakirev had been dismissed because of the radical nature of his programmes. Indeed, early in their correspondence he had upbraided Tchaikovsky for not being sufficiently acquainted with 'modern music'. But Balakirev was wrong there. Tchaikovsky's acquaintance with modern music, though not so extensive as that of the Petersburg master, was quite sufficient for him to be able to please the more radical Balakirev if he were not at the same time trying to please Anton Rubinstein.

[32]EU, p. 85.
[33]RA, p. 132.
[34]EU, p. 86.

3

The complete nationalist (1869–74)

The idea of an overture on the subject of Romeo and Juliet was suggested to Tchaikovsky by Balakirev during a visit he made to Moscow in the autumn of 1869. In a letter dated 4/16 October – after his return to Petersburg – Balakirev reproves Tchaikovsky for his inactivity which is a result of 'lack of concentration' and gives him a vigorous prod: 'Just at the moment, thinking about you and the overture, an idea has come to me involuntarily. I seem to feel that it should open with a fierce *allegro*, representing a clash of swords, rather like this:

Ex. 3

'If I were composing the overture, I should become enthusiastic over this germ, I should brood over it, or to put it better, I should turn it over in my mind, until there is a possibility of something vital springing from these roots.'[1]

[1]EU, pp. 92–3.

28

Tchaikovsky did brood over the germ, though his overture is in four-four time. He does use sharp chordal sword-thrusts and much of his semiquaver passage-work bears some resemblance to Balakirev's, which itself resembles certain passages in his own *King Lear* overture (which Tchaikovsky knew), especially in the developmental storm section. Such passage-work, of course, is fairly commonplace and too much should not be made of resemblances. But there are many other features of the overture which show the profound influence of Balakirev. The first subject, for instance, after only fourteen bars, develops in typical Balakirev canonic fashion:

Ex. 4

Tchaikovsky had borrowed the score of a work by Balakirev published earlier the same year, the Musical Picture, *1000 years*[2] (a

[2]RA, p. 139.

revised version of the *Second Overture on Russian Themes* later to be further revised as the Symphonic Poem *Russia*) which abounds in such bustling canonic devices, and Tchaikovsky was taking great care to please the older man. Of the superb second subject Balakirev wrote to him on 1/13 December, by which time the overture had been finished: 'It is simply fascinating. I often play it and should like to hug you for it. In it is the tenderness and longing of love, and much more that ought to go straight to the heart of the immoral Albrecht. When I play this I visualize you wallowing in your bath with Artôt-Padilla herself rubbing your tummy ardently with fragrant soap-suds.'[3] Rimsky-Korsakov later wrote that it was one of the best themes in the whole of Russian music and Stassov was moved to remark: 'There used to be five of you; now there are six.'[4] The only misgivings Balakirev had were that Romeo and Juliet were 'Europeans, not Persians', but the beautiful corollary to the theme drew from him nothing but praise: 'You have done something new and you have done it well — the alternating chords over a pedal-point, a little *à la* Russlan.'[5] It is perhaps not entirely fortuitous that the second subject of Balakirev's *King Lear* overture has repeated alternating chords at the end of the first phrase. In the development section of *Romeo and Juliet* the two chords alternate even more in the manner of the seminal passage in Glinka's opera *Russlan and Ludmilla* to which Balakirev referred — the sudden magical disappearance of Ludmilla near the beginning of the opera. Incidentally it might not be entirely idle to speculate how much such passages, including the rather different opening of the Coronation Scene in Mussorgsky's *Boris Godunov*, which was being composed at this very time, were originally indebted to the alternating chords at the blessing of the daggers in Act IV of Meyerbeer's *Les Huguenots*.

The first performance of this version of the overture was given by Nicholas Rubinstein in Moscow the following March. It went unnoticed. Rubinstein himself was impressed, however, and persuaded Bote & Bock in Berlin to publish it. Tchaikovsky revised it for publication in accordance with Balakirev's advice, substituting a new introduction for a theme which Balakirev bluntly stated had 'neither beauty nor strength', but the conclusion of the revised score displeased

[3] *ibid.*, p. 146.
[4] *ibid.*, p. 151.
[5] EU, p. 97.

him: 'Why those sudden thumped chords in the very last bars? This is contrary to the meaning of the drama.'[6]

As well as the introduction, extensive passages in the *Allegro giusto* where the introductory themes are employed had to be altered. As far as structure is concerned, not only does the type of sonata form employed by Tchaikovsky derive directly from Balakirev's *King Lear* overture and Musical Picture *1000 years*, but the latter work provides the obvious prototype for the incorporation of introductory materials, foreign to the main subjects of the *Allegro*, into the development and recapitulation – a formula which Tchaikovsky was to use even more successfully in the first movement of his next symphony.

Another very important way in which Tchaikovsky is indebted to Balakirev in this overture is in the semitonal relationships of keys. In Balakirev's *King Lear* overture, in B♭ minor, the second subject is in D major, recapitulated in D♭ major. In *Romeo and Juliet*, in B minor, the second subject is in D♭ major, recapitulated in D major. (In Balakirev's *1000 years*, which is in D major, the second subject is in B♭ minor, recapitulated in B minor.) There are other semitonal repetitions of themes which bear Balakirev's imprint no less emphatically than similar passages in the music of Borodin and Rimsky-Korsakov. Also the orchestration is the reverse of garish and crude. Balakirev's stern displeasure at these very faults in *Fatum* were responsible for Tchaikovsky's much more economical scoring here. Even in the 'crude' finish a timpani roll is the only form of percussion employed. This is all very different to his methods in, say, the finale of the Fourth Symphony with its interminable ear-splitting strokes of the cymbals and bass drum.

While he was still working on the first version of *Romeo and Juliet* in the autumn of 1869 Tchaikovsky completed an arrangement for piano duet of Fifty Russian Folk-Songs for his publisher, Jurgenson. Other work for Jurgenson and Bessel at this time included piano pot-pourris on Meyerbeer's *Pardon de Ploërmel* and his own *Voyevoda*, and piano arrangements of such works as Anton Rubinstein's Musical Picture, *Ivan the Terrible*. Much more important, however, was the completion of the first group of songs he was to publish, his Opus 6.

In the late eighteen-sixties and early seventies Russian song perhaps reached its zenith both in the unparalleled beauty of the music and the apposite setting of texts not only appropriate but often of exquisite poetic quality. Together with Glinka and Dargomyzhsky, whose best

[6] *ibid.*

songs revealed penetrating insight combined with subtle declamation, Balakirev had earlier established an ideal with his first group of twenty songs of which Tchaikovsky later declared himself to be passionately fond. In their wake came the extraordinary outpouring of songs of the Petersburg group – Borodin, Mussorgsky and Rimsky-Korsakov. The half-dozen songs Borodin wrote between 1867 and 1870 are miniature masterpieces. The Petersburg composers' essential lack of theoretical knowledge is nowhere more vital than in these songs of Borodin, where the almost impressionistic melodic and harmonic use of the whole-tone scale, unresolved seconds and so on, adds immeasurably to their strange beauty. But they were much criticized for their 'ugliness' at the time, as were Mussorgsky's for much the same reasons. Both these composers possessed the almost unique ability to compose words and music as a simultaneous act of creation. All but one of the Borodin songs under review were settings of his own texts, as were many of Mussorgsky's.

Common to most of the Russian song-writers of the period, including Tchaikovsky, was the influence of Schumann's songs. But on two vital counts Tchaikovsky in his songs cannot be compared with his Petersburg contemporaries. First, their literary taste was impeccable, his was at best variable. Secondly, Tchaikovsky's Conservatoire training precluded any possibility of his writing 'novel' and consequently 'incorrect' harmonies, resulting in the comparative tameness of his inspiration in his songs.

Cui hauled Tchaikovsky over the coals on the first count, ridiculing the declamation in 'Not a word, O my friend' (Op. 6, No. 2) and alleging that Tchaikovsky regarded the text with 'despotic presumption', repeating words at will in order to suit the musical phrase.[7] Of course many composers have treated texts in this way while at the same time writing excellent music, but Cui's criticisms could be more readily dismissed if no direct comparisons with Tchaikovsky's contemporaries had perforce to be made. Tchaikovsky's lack of literary taste was not so important in his better operas, since the effect of relatively poor manipulation of the text was made up for and even eliminated by his subjective feeling for his characters, which could be movingly depicted in the score, the words being merely appropriate pegs upon which to hang the music. Tchaikovsky was later to appreciate the nature of the original *Queen of Spades* by Pushkin so little that his libretto, by his equally tasteless brother, was a sentimental travesty of

[7]ER (9), pp. 197–8.

the ironic original. But this does not matter, since the opera can be taken on its own terms. Tchaikovsky's greatest opera, also based on a Pushkin work, *Eugene Onegin*, is much closer to the spirit of the original, but even here Turgenyev, rather unkindly, found it incumbent upon himself to write scathingly to Tolstoy, after praising the music: 'But what a libretto!'[8]

On the second count Tchaikovsky's songs compare even less favourably with those of Mussorgsky and Borodin. His compliance with the established drawing-room norm, while it resulted in the immediate popularity of some of his songs, such as his setting of a Russian translation of Goethe's 'Nur wer die Sehnsucht kennt' (Op. 6, No. 6), at the same time deprived the vast majority of them of that crucial ounce of emotional energy which might weigh in their favour against the charge of shallow sentimentality. It is this very type of sentimentality upon which Mussorgsky wrote such a gentle skit in the middle section of his song 'The Hobby Horse' from the Nursery Cycle. Furthermore Tchaikovsky's harmonic ordinariness reflects a trivial preoccupation with a correctness which he felt to be necessary in a *salon* piece, whether for voice and piano or for piano solo, in contradistinction to his attitude to the setting of folk-song, in which on the contrary he felt that such correctness would be ill placed. It is in his original songs, rather than in his adaptation of folk-music to symphonic use, that he falls considerably below the standards of the Petersburg composers. This has manifestly nothing to do with whether he or they were more, or less, 'nationalist' composers, but it certainly is a result of the difference in their musical education.

All the same, everything in these early songs is not on the debit side. In spite of Cui's strictures, 'Not a word, O my friend' reveals some aspects of Tchaikovsky's later lyrical style, for example in *Eugene Onegin*, as does 'To forget so soon', a song without opus number composed soon afterwards. The beginnings of Tchaikovsky's gift of identifying himself with the emotions of his characters are here revealed, resulting in a sincerity conspicuously lacking in most of the others, particularly 'Nur wer die Sehnsucht kennt'.

Tchaikovsky still had rooms with Nicholas Rubinstein, who had recently moved to a larger house. In spite of the noisy gaiety with which Rubinstein surrounded himself, Tchaikovsky was able to entertain his own friends. Balakirev had visited him much in the autumn of 1869,

[8]RN, p. 192.

taking Borodin with him on one occasion.[9] And when he and Rimsky-Korsakov visited Moscow in January 1870 they 'naturally' called on Tchaikovsky 'every day'. They considered him now to be one of themselves, and besides praising *Romeo and Juliet* Rimsky-Korsakov dedicated a song to him.[10] (Tchaikovsky reciprocated the compliment a couple of years later, dedicating one song of his Op. 16 to the newly wedded composer and another, a charming cradle song, to his young bride.) But Tchaikovsky was not really happy in his domestic life. He wrote to Sasha on 5/17 February[11] that there was nobody in Moscow with whom he could enter into a 'really intimate domestic relationship. I often think how happy I'd be if you lived here, or at least if there was somebody like you.' He longed for the noise of children in the house, 'in a word, for family life'. He told her that he was about to begin his 'third' opera based on Lazhechnikov's tragedy *The Oprichnik*, and that two piano pieces were being published, one dedicated to her. This was a *Valse-Scherzo*, Op. 7; the other was *Capriccio*, Op. 8 – both trivial, as were the three pieces of Op. 9, 'Rêverie', 'Salon Polka' and 'Salon Mazurka', composed later the same year. The letter ends with further remarks about his malaise.

Work on *The Oprichnik* was interrupted by his receiving a summons to Paris, where his dear friend Vladimir Shilovsky was desperately ill. But Shilovsky was soon well enough to be removed to a resort near Frankfurt-am-Main where they were 'very bored'.[12] Tchaikovsky did no work whatever, but he visited Mannheim for the Beethoven Centenary Festival and was much impressed by the D major Mass. On another occasion he went to Wiesbaden to find Nicholas Rubinstein, compulsive gambler that he was, quite sure that he would break the bank at roulette, 'losing his last rouble' in the process. They all scurried over the border to Switzerland at the outbreak of the Franco-Prussian war in July. After six weeks at Interlaken, where Tchaikovsky was intoxicated by the scenery, and Shilovsky's health improved, he returned to Russia in a desultory fashion by way of Munich and Vienna.[13]

He had been working on the revised version of *Romeo and Juliet* which Balakirev was unable to perform himself in St Petersburg since, for financial reasons, there were no Free School concerts in the 1870–1 season. Work on *The Oprichnik* was rather half-heartedly resumed,

[9] *ibid.*, pp. 62–3.
[10] RL, p. 61.
[11] RI, Vol. V, pp. 203–4.
[12] RN, p. 70.
[13] *ibid.*, p. 71.

but was laid aside in favour of a string quartet, started early in 1871. He was not really interested in chamber music, but he was short of funds and hoped to raise a little money by giving an entire concert of his own compositions. So chamber music, songs and piano music it had to be. 'Nur wer die Sehnsucht kennt' was inevitably included, as were other songs from Op. 6 together with 'So soon forgotten', an aria from *The Voyevoda* and piano pieces from Op. 9 played by Nicholas Rubinstein. But the newly composed String Quartet in D major, with the beautiful *Andante cantabile* slow movement, based on a folk-song he had heard at Kamenka, was the major work in the programme. With this composition, hardly less than with *Romeo and Juliet*, Tchaikovsky's first maturity is fully established. Although new to him, the medium is brilliantly exploited and his predilection for, and mastery of, the technique of writing for strings is demonstrated beyond doubt. More than this, the style is indubitably his own. For example, the second subject of the first movement is differentiated from the first not only in character but, much more important, in speed; the recapitulation of the first subject is accompanied by skirls on the first violin derived from previous material; a delicate new subject acts as a foil to the folk-song in the *Andante cantabile*, a movement of charming simplicity not unworthy of a composer who later was to some extent influenced by Tchaikovsky's quartets – Dvořák. And the trio has a syncopated sprightliness in Borodin's manner – indeed it was possibly as a result of Tchaikovsky's success in the field that Borodin decided to try his hand at it himself three or four years later, much to Balakirev's disgust, for Balakirev held the view that modern composers were no longer able to exploit the worn-out medium of chamber music.

The concert took place on 16/28 March with great success, not diminished by the attendance of Turgenyev, although he arrived too late to hear the quartet. Tchaikovsky started again on *The Oprichnik* with renewed enthusiasm, but his work was interrupted by a round of summer visits, first to Kiev to collect Anatol and take him to Kamenka, where he composed a ballet for Sasha's children whom he adored. The ballet was called *Swan Lake*. Next he visited his friend N. D. Kondratyev at Nizy, also in the Ukraine, where he completed a text-book on harmony soon to be used by Rimsky-Korsakov, who was still ignorant of these matters. Finally he went to the Shilovsky estate at Ussovo where he was 'tenderly' cared for, as he wrote to Anatol,[14]

[14]RI, Vol. V, p. 258.

taking up again work on *The Oprichnik*. He allowed Shilovsky to compose and orchestrate the introduction to Act II, almost certainly during this visit. This was the time of their greatest intimacy. The wealthy Shilovsky was fairly free with his money. But Tchaikovsky kept exact details of his obligations and eight years later was able to refute rumours put about by Shilovsky, from whom he was by then estranged, that he had lent Tchaikovsky '28,000 roubles'. But for the next five years he visited Ussovo each summer.

On his return to Moscow he was at last able to move out of Nicholas Rubinstein's house and take a small three-room flat of his own, where he would have peace to compose. He also engaged a servant, M. I. Sofronov, who had previously been in the employment of his colleague the violinist Ferdinand Laub.[15] N. A. Hubert took his place in the Rubinstein household. Hubert also succeeded Laroche as the music critic of *Sovremennaya Letopis*, sharing the job with Kashkin and Tchaikovsky, who needed every extra rouble he could get to meet his considerably increased expenses. When *Sovremennaya Letopis* suspended publication he contributed reviews to *Russkiye Vyedomosti*. Rather interestingly, in December, in a review of Schumann's Fourth Symphony, he remarked upon its colourless orchestration, and told Klimenko that he was thinking of re-orchestrating it himself.[16] Meanwhile his resumed work on *The Oprichnik*, which he had seemed determined to finish by the end of the year, was again interrupted by Vladimir Shilovsky, who invited him to go on a month's trip to Nice at his expense. It is possibly understandable that Tchaikovsky was anxious that everybody except Rubinstein should be made to think that he had gone to his sister's at Kamenka, as he wrote to Anatol on 2/14 December.[17]

Immediately on his return at the end of January/beginning of February 1872, he composed a Festival Cantata commissioned for a Polytechnic Exhibition to be held a month or two later, not as a labour of love but because of the 750-rouble fee; but at length, in spite of all these interruptions, he finished *The Oprichnik* in May and sent off the score to Nápravník, who in February had given the first Petersburg performance of *Romeo and Juliet*. Even Cui, whose reviews were becoming increasingly curmudgeonly to friend and foe alike, was enthusiastic about the overture and wrote that it was a 'talented

---

[15]RH, Vol. I, p. 372. M. I. Sofronov was soon to be succeeded by his brother, A. I. Sofronov.
[16]RN, p. 73.
[17]RI, Vol. V, p. 265.

composition'.[18] But *The Oprichnik* was not finally accepted for performance at the Maryinsky until the end of the year, and it did not receive its first performance until 1874.

Tchaikovsky had got the itch to go abroad out of his system by his visit to Nice, and spent a quiet and untroubled summer at Kamenka, Nizy and Ussovo, writing a charming Second Symphony in C minor which was completed and orchestrated in the autumn. In this work, as in his next opera, *Vakula the Smith*, he came closer than Mussorgsky ever did to the actual music, if not to the cultural ideals, of Balakirev, and indeed some of his music at this time, particularly in the opera, is so like Balakirev as to be almost indistinguishable from the original. The symphony is entirely original none the less, even if the structure of the first movement is indebted to Balakirev's Musical Picture *1000 years*. A Ukrainian variant of the Russian folk-song 'Down by Mother Volga', which introduces and closes the movement, is also used as an integral part of the development section in the *Allegro commodo* in much the same way as the initial folk-tune in Balakirev's work. The two main subjects of the *Allegro commodo* are not folk-like, for Balakirev would not have approved of this in the first movement of a symphony. Incessant modulation, a pronounced feature of Balakirev's music at the time, is also one of the features of this original version of the movement[19] (it was later to be revised). Its graceful and inventive lyricism was not to please Tchaikovsky later, but it is disarming all the same.

The opening of 'Down by Mother Volga' is worth quoting (Ex. 5(a)), since this kind of theme with its typical drop of a fourth pervaded Tchaikovsky's music not only in earlier years (compare with Ex. 2 on p. 21) but also for the rest of his life. Quoted also is the opening of (b) the motto theme from the *Manfred* symphony (1885); (c) Francesca's main subject from *Francesca da Rimini* (1876); (d) the first theme of *Hamlet* (1888) (see examples on page 38).

In the First Symphony Tchaikovsky had used the *Scherzo* of his discarded early piano sonata. He was always loath to waste material. For the slow movement here he makes use of the bridal march from Act III of the opera *Undina*, and its form, *ABACABA*, is explained by the opera plot; for the hero's wedding keeps being interrupted by Undina's emissaries. The Raff-like nature of the nuptial march is

---

[18] RN, p. 79.
[19] The first and second subjects of the original version are quoted in Gerald Abraham's foreword to the Eulenburg miniature score (EQ), pp. vii and viii.

deliciously offset by a typically lyrical second subject over a dominant pedal, while the central C section is a variant of No. 6 of Fifty Russian Folk-Songs, 'Spin, O my spinner'. This song receives a considerable amount of development in various orchestral guises and makes a perfect centre section to the little symmetrical movement. This is Tchaikovsky's first excursion into the realm of the symphonic march, innocent indeed in comparison with some of his later examples.

Ex. 5

He does not employ the valse in this symphony, but using the scherzo and trio of Borodin's First Symphony as a prototype he equals the 'mighty handful' and produces the 'folk-like' trio of which Balakirev was such a firm advocate. But it was with the finale that Tchaikovsky most enraptured the Petersburg group, as he wrote later to Modest: 'When I was in Petersburg I played the finale at a musical evening at Rimsky-Korsakov's flat, and the whole company all but tore me to pieces in their enthusiasm.'[20] The Ukrainian folk-song 'The Crane' is treated, in the manner of Glinka's *Kamarinskaya*, to a series of changing background orchestral variations of tremendous virtuosity. The very ordinary and square-cut nature of the theme itself allows

[20]RI, Vol. V, p. 303, letter of 13/25 February 1873.

much more satisfactory development than if it had been 'sufficient unto itself', as it were, and allows Tchaikovsky to introduce a beautiful off-beat lilting second subject as a foil. The increasingly close juxtaposition of these two themes produces a suitably exciting *presto* climax, and the humorous introduction of the whole-tone scale in one of the variations adds to the general high spirits. This finale is in C major, so that the idea adumbrated by Beethoven in his C minor symphony of strife-to-victory, which the Romantics were so fond of, is here employed by Tchaikovsky – and in exactly the same keys as Beethoven. There is as much folk-like material in this symphony as in any other Russian symphony, and folk-song is at the very core of the work. It is more central than in Rimsky-Korsakov's or Borodin's first symphonies, or either of Balakirev's. Although Mussorgsky had to write a symphonic *Allegro* for Balakirev, his heart was not in it and he failed ever to write a satisfactory symphonic movement. The only work with which Tchaikovsky's symphony can be compared in this respect is Borodin's Second Symphony in B minor, the composition of which had already begun. Although Borodin may not use genuine folk-songs in this masterpiece, the question may be asked whether he has penetrated to the very heart of Russian folk-music much more successfully than Tchaikovsky in his Second Symphony.

To answer this question affirmatively would be to misunderstand the nature of the influence of folk-music upon the two composers. In his B minor Symphony, as in the opera *Prince Igor*, Borodin's superb lyrical gift blossomed most successfully – though not exclusively – under the influence of two particular types of folk-song: the epic *bylina*, the kind of heroic ballad sung by the bards of old, of a type first introduced successfully by Glinka at the beginning of *Russlan and Ludmilla*; and the Caucasian or Crimean Tartar type of melody (Borodin had royal Caucasian ancestors), sometimes referred to as 'oriental', which Balakirev had so ably exploited in his *Song of Georgia* and his Piano Fantasy *Islamey*. Tchaikovsky did not attempt to use *bylini*-like materials in his symphonies, though he used them in the manner of Glinka in *Vakula the Smith*. But he was never successful with 'oriental' folk-songs from the periphery of the Russian empire. He did not often attempt to use such exotic material in the manipulation of which Balakirev, Borodin and Rimsky-Korsakov were consummate masters, but when he did, as in the song 'The Canary' (1874), he failed miserably. It was when he used rhythmically simple folk-songs from the Western provinces of the Russian empire, whether foot-stamping as in the finale of the symphony, or lyrically nostalgic or whatever, that he matched the 'mighty handful'. It may be that Tchaikovsky's Second Symphony is inferior to Borodin's. But if it is, it is certainly not because the particular folk-intonations used in it are in any way inferior to Borodin's, only different. If Tchaikovsky's charming symphony does not probe the psychological depths in the manner of his later symphonies, this does not necessarily mean that it is inferior.

It was at Christmas time that he visited St Petersburg and charmed the 'mighty handful' with the symphony. His real reason for going to the capital was to play through *The Oprichnik* to the final committee, who unanimously approved. Before returning to Moscow he asked Stassov, who had gone into ecstasies over his symphony, to suggest a subject for a symphonic fantasia. Stassov suggested Gogol's *Taras Bulba*, *Ivanhoe* or Shakespeare's *The Tempest*. For the latter he gave him a detailed programme. In his letter of thanks from Moscow, Tchaikovsky praised the programme and called it 'enticing and inspiring',[21] but he did not start work on it for some time, as he was commissioned to write incidental music for a production in May of Ostrovsky's fairy-tale play *Snow Maiden*, probably as a result of the enormous success of the first performance of the Second Symphony in Moscow on 26 January/7 February 1873. A great deal of music had to be hurriedly got together for *Snow Maiden*, which even included some singing characters and a chorus. As it turned out, the delightful music was more successful with the public than the play itself, but his intention of expanding it into an opera was eventually forestalled by Rimsky-Korsakov, whose charming work owes a great deal to the Tchaikovsky of the early seventies.[22] He received a fee of 350 roubles. His annual salary at the Conservatoire had now risen to 2,302 roubles, and together with fees for compositions, articles and so on would have amounted to quite a comfortable income had not his financial affairs been in a haphazard state. As it was, when he was in a financially sound condition he was always apt to give money away, or to fritter it away on another trip to western Europe, which he now proceeded to do after short visits to Nizy and Kamenka, visiting Germany – where he joined the Jurgenson family – Switzerland, Italy and France. During this holiday he started a diary which he kept fitfully over the years.[23] Many of the entries were destroyed after his death by Modest. What remains is of some interest to a biographer, certainly, but a great

[21] RI, Vol. V, p. 299.
[22] For a detailed discussion of the incidental music to *Snow Maiden*, and a comparison with Rimsky-Korsakov, see EO(2), pp. 133–6.
[23] RG.

deal of it is quite frankly rather dull. Tchaikovsky's best writing is in his letters. All the same here and there the diary is illuminating and it certainly confirms beyond doubt not only his homosexuality, which he refers to by means of a private symbol, but his feelings of over-whelming guilt about it with periodic remarks such as: 'Oh! what a monster of a person I am.'

When Tchaikovsky returned to Russia at the beginning of August he went immediately to Ussovo, where for a blissfully happy two weeks he sketched out *The Tempest* and enjoyed the Russian countryside to the full – alone. Years later he wrote of his intense joy during those two weeks, wandering alone in the woods and valleys, listening at night to the sounds of nature by an open window. *The Tempest* seemed to write itself.[24] Shilovsky's absence in Moscow was the *sine qua non* of this blissful happiness, for his presence had an unsettling effect upon the composer, who was in any case beginning to tire of his company. He returned to Moscow at the beginning of September and quickly completed the orchestration of *The Tempest*, which he dedicated to Stassov. He moved twice within the space of three months, wrote reviews of operas, resumed his 'boring' classes at the Conservatoire and corresponded with the publisher Bessel about a piano reduction of *The Oprichnik*, due to appear at the time of the first performance, which was now finally arranged for the spring of 1874.

He continued to have periodic bouts of moodiness and self-pity. He wrote to Modest at the end of November/beginning of December that although he dined frequently at Shilovsky's his society weighed heavily upon him and there was no one who was really close to him.[25] Yet just as often he was elated. He was learning English in order to be able to read Dickens – especially *The Pickwick Papers* – in the original. The exuberant early fruits of these labours are to be found in a letter he had written to Sasha and Modest at Kamenka the previous April:

My good sister and my dear brother!
    I have know what mötsch plesir that you learn the Englisch language; böt you cannot told that I cannot understand. I kan understand wery biutiföll oll what you will and enough bether. My brother! You are one fulischmen, böt you, my dear sister, are one biutiföll women. I have not times to scrive this letter englisch, böt God sawe the Quenn and collection

[24]RK, Vol. I, pp. 307–8.
[25]RI, Vol. V, p. 335.

of Britisch autors is one trifles ... Do not argue withe me, You argue against reason and i abide by what I say...

    I are your
        affectioned brother
           Pither.[26]

The first performance of *The Tempest*, on 7/19 December, was so triumphantly successful that, like the Second Symphony the previous season, it had to be repeated at another concert. Stassov's programme, to which he adhered strictly, is satisfactorily symmetrical: the sea at the beginning and the end; the magician Prospero second and penultimately; and the central Ariel and Caliban section enveloped on either side by the love theme of Miranda and Ferdinand. Only the short storm section, which precedes the initial halting representation of the love theme, might seem to upset the balance, but this is offset by the correspondingly stormy passionate nature of the second version of the love theme after the Ariel and Caliban section. Why, then, is the work not really successful? The answer partially lies in its rather hodge-podge nature. Tchaikovsky had told Rimsky-Korsakov that he was going to use the Prelude to *Das Rheingold*, constructed on a single triad, as his model for depicting the sea, but Rimsky did not think that there was much in common between Tchaikovsky's sea and Wagner's river.[27] None the less passages at the opening and close of *The Tempest* are Wagerian – as Rimsky-Korsakov acknowledged. Other discernible influences are Liszt, for example in the repetitive nature of the phrases in the storm section, Balakirev in some of the harmonies, and even Glinka in some magical wind passages before the storm. None of these influences would matter in the least if there were enough subjective material of Tchaikovsky's own to counter-balance them. The characteristic love-theme itself is not powerful enough to make up for what is essentially a colourless atmosphere, though in this fact itself there is a certain resemblance to the Liszt of the symphonic poems. In his next programme work, *Francesca da Rimini*, he solved these problems, absorbed his influences – including Wagner – and produced a much greater, because more subjective, work.

At the beginning of 1874 Tchaikovsky must have been well satisfied with his position as a composer. The Second Symphony and *The Tempest* had been outstandingly successful. At last *The Oprichnik* was going to be produced, though he had trouble with the censor and the

[26] *ibid.*, pp. 314–15.
[27] RD, pp. 172–3.

conductor Nápravník had been considerably freer with his blue pencil than he would have liked. On a visit to Russia the well-known pianist Hans von Bülow praised his music and performed the Variations for piano from Op. 19, composed the previous autumn.[28] A second String Quartet, in F major, Op. 22, dedicated to the Grand Duke Constantine Nicholayevich and first performed in March, was instantly successful. It had previously been given a private performance at a musical evening at Nicholas Rubinstein's. Nicholas had to be away, but Anton was present on that occasion.[29] He disliked the quartet, and to Tchaikovsky's chagrin remained one of the few leading musicians in Russia still to doubt Tchaikovsky's real ability.

[28] RN, p. 102.
[29] RB(1), p. 84.

4

Nationalist operas (1874)

At the end of March Tchaikovsky went to St Petersburg to be present at the rehearsals of *The Oprichnik*. He stayed at his father's house. Nine years earlier his father had married a comfortable motherly woman of no accomplishment, who admirably ministered to the needs of the old man – much to the envy of his son, who himself ardently desired a somewhat younger version of his stepmother for a wife. He was beginning to have grave doubts about *The Oprichnik*. On 25 March/6 April he wrote to his pupil Sergei Taneyev: 'To tell the truth, there's nothing particularly good in this opera, and I shouldn't like you to come up to Petersburg just for it.'[1] However, not only Taneyev but nearly the whole staff of the Moscow Conservatoire did come, including Nicholas Rubinstein. The first performance was on 12/24 April, less than three months after the first performance of Mussorgsky's *Boris Godunov*, and some fifteen months after the première of Rimsky-Korsakov's *Maid of Pskov* which, like *The Oprichnik*, is about the reign of Boris Godunov's predecessor Ivan the Terrible. The greatest of these three nationalist operas is *Boris Godunov*. Rimsky-Korsakov's and Tchaikovsky's best folk or folkish music – Tchaikovsky's nearly all lifted bodily from *The Voyevoda* – is employed and harmonized charmingly but decoratively in the fresco-like Balakirev manner – eminently appropriate, but diametrically opposed to the simple, stark, startling bareness of Mussorgsky's extraordinary penetration of the folk idiom. With the exception of Stassov, no one really understood *Boris*. Balakirev made 'cutting remarks' about it, Borodin told his wife. Cui tore it to shreds in an article. Rimsky-Korsakov's attitude to it may be gauged by the fact that some twenty years later he issued an adulterated edition with 'corrected' harmonies, smoothed-out 'roughnesses', numerous cuts, inserted bars to balance the formal structure and a complete revision of the 'inept' instrumentation. Tchaikovsky, therefore, was hardly alone in his opinion, emphatically

[1] RF(1), p. 3.

44

expressed in a letter to Modest after he had thoroughly studied the score: 'With all my heart and soul I send Mussorgsky's music to the Devil: it is the most banal, base parody of music.'[2] That Tchaikovsky's attempts at realism are hardly more successful than Rimsky-Korsakov's is not surprising if one takes into account his temporary views on the subject, expressed in a letter some three years later: 'Realism undoubtedly implies a certain narrow-mindedness, an ability to satisfy very easily and cheaply the thirst for a knowledge of *truth* ... The realist is sceptical towards those who seek *reconciliation* with life in religion, in philosophy, in *art*.'[3]

His attitude to opera is very well summed up in another letter:

In composing an opera, the composer must constantly think of the stage, i.e. not forget that the theatre needs not only melodies and harmonies but action to hold the attention of the theatre-goer who has come to hear *and see* – finally, that the style of theatre music must correspond to the style of scene-painting: simple, clear and colourful. Just as a picture by Meissonier would lose all its charm if it were put on the stage, so would rich music, full of harmonic subtleties, lose a great deal in the theatre, for there the listener needs sharply drawn melodies against a transparent harmonic background.

Not only had *The Voyevoda* been unsuccessful, but of the ensuing, fairy-tale operas one had been flatly rejected by the committee and the other abandoned because of the unsuitability of the libretto. Tchaikovsky's next opera had to be a stage success:

The stage often paralyses the composer's musical inspiration, so that symphonic and chamber music stand far higher than operatic music. A symphony or sonata imposes on me no limitations; on the other hand opera possesses the advantage that it gives the possibility to speak in the musical language of the masses. An opera may be given forty times in one season, a symphony perhaps once in ten years.[4]

Despite all this, the most beautiful music in *The Oprichnik* is taken from *The Voyevoda*. Particularly lovely is the chorus of maidens based on Ostrovsky's folk-tune and the *khorovod* of girls – transferred from the finale of Act II of *The Voyevoda* – at the end of Act I, from which the following is an extract:

[2]RI, Vol. V, p. 372, letter of 29 October/10 November 1874.
[3]RK, Vol. I, p. 89.
[4]RI, Vol. VIII, p. 445; EO(2), p. 117 (Gerald Abraham's translation).

Ex. 6

Only thirteen pages of the vocal score of Act I[5] consist of newly composed music, and a great deal of this has a flavour of Meyerbeer. Take, for example, Natalya's *arioso* in G♭ major, *con passione largamente*, which, as Gerald Abraham has pointed out, is the key of 'Tu l'as dit' from Act IV of *Les Huguenots*.[6] In both are to be found *tremolando* strings, the echoing of the voice by a solo instrument and so on (but the actual melody is totally different). Many subsequent operas of Tchaikovsky employ a similar aria in G♭ major at some vital point in the drama and, as is shown later, he also became spiritually soaked in the haunting melody of Meyerbeer's masterly love duet, which was a favourite with the audiences of the day. The orchestral postlude in Tchaikovsky's *arioso* typically oscillates between the chords of the tonic and the 'Russian' sixth. Not so happy are the other Meyerbeerian features, such as the tawdry conventional horror depicted at the end of the opera or the introduction to Act III, though towards the close of this *entr'acte* the following passage (Ex. 7(a)), curiously bears a close resemblance to Yaroslavna's theme from Igor's aria in Borodin's *Prince Igor* (Ex. 7(b)), which itself resembles a theme from the opera *Mlada* (Ex. 7(c)), composed collectively by Cui, Mussorgsky, Rimsky-Korsakov and Borodin at the same time as Tchaikovsky was putting the finishing touches to *The Oprichnik*.

Igor's aria did not take its final form until the early eighties, and it

[5] The vocal score of *The Oprichnik* referred to is Vol. 34 of *Polnoe Sobranie Sochineny* (Moscow, 1959).
[6] EO(2), p. 130.

Ex. 7

could be that this melody was constructed from possibly subconscious memories of both the *Mlada* and *Oprichnik* passages, since it seems to be a coalescence of the two.

Besides one or two reminiscence motives, there is an important recurring theme depicting the Oprichniks, the dreaded bodyguard of Ivan the Terrible. As we have seen, only a few months before starting work on the opera Tchaikovsky had made a piano-duet arrangement of Anton Rubinstein's Musical Picture *Ivan the Terrible* for Bessel,[7] and the origin of his motive is the military theme from Rubinstein's work. For at last Anton Rubinstein had come off his high horse and like every other Russian composer of any note had jumped on the 'folk' band-wagon. Balakirev had given the first performance of the Rubinstein 'Picture'. Borodin thought it had moments of 'real power'. The second subject is distinctly folkish, though not nearly so successful as some of Rubinstein's later efforts in the same vein – for example the opening melody of his Symphony in G minor. Tchaikovsky's recurring motive is much used, but only in the last three acts. This happens more or less to fit in with the drama, since the hero Andrey does not become an Oprichnik until Act II; but the main reason for it is that Act I, having mostly been transferred from *The Voyevoda*, was composed before the theme had been thought of and in a very different context.

The opera tends therefore to be a rather patchy affair: Tchaikovsky even managed to make use of material rescued from *Fatum* in the duet of Natalya and Andrey in the last act. But the first act does not have a monopoly of the successful music. The wedding chorus in Act IV is racy, Natalya's *arioso* in Act III foreshadows some of the best of Tatyana's music in *Eugene Onegin*, and Andrey, just before his admission to the band of Oprichniks in Act II, scene 2, has a splendid aria in a typically individual Tchaikovsky mould. Dramatically this scene is the finest in the opera. It consists of three elements: the dignified ecclesiastical chant of the Oprichniks (who are pseudo-monks), which is similar to the opening theme of *Romeo and Juliet*; the conventional Meyerbeerian stagey passages allotted to Basmanov, Vyazminsky and the Oprichniks when they are not chanting; and Andrey's own comments on the proceedings and thoughts of the past in his lovely passages. The alternation and gradual build-up of these materials is both theatrically and structurally effective; but Tchaikovsky was to

[7]RN, p. 63.

achieve total success in the manipulation of such materials only in *The Queen of Spades*.

The Oprichnik achieved a moderate success in spite of the composer's immediate dissatisfaction with it. It was periodically revived, much to the composer's later dismay, since he wanted to recompose 'two-thirds' of it, but was unable to do so as he had parted with all his rights to Bessel. Rimsky-Korsakov, however, had not parted with his rights, and his almost equally immediate dissatisfaction with his own opera resulted in a complete reworking not long afterwards. He eventually revised it a second time, and this third version was first performed in 1895. It was soon after this that he felt it incumbent upon himself to undertake the revision of *Boris*.

On the night of the first performance of *The Oprichnik* Tchaikovsky went to a gala supper in his honour, at which to his surprise he received the M.A. Kondratyev Prize of 300 roubles. Then, in response to a commission from his paper to write a review of a performance of *A Life for the Tsar* in Milan, he gladly left for Italy on 14/26 April. After seeing the sights in Venice, Rome, Naples and Florence, he returned in disgust to Russia at the beginning of May on learning that *A Life for the Tsar* was to be postponed to allow for alterations to 'suit the taste of the Italian public'.[8]

At the beginning of June, immediately after the end of term at the Conservatoire, he hastened to N. D. Kondratyev's at Nizy and started work on a new opera. At the behest of the Grand Duchess Helena Pavlovna, Polonsky had prepared for her protégé Serov a libretto based on one of Gogol's Ukrainian tales, *Christmas Eve*. Serov's untimely death had left her with a libretto but no composer. This was in 1871. Some time afterwards she decided to offer prizes for the best two settings, and the winning work was also to be performed at the Maryinsky Theatre. The Russian Musical Society had to take over the competition when she herself died in 1873. The closing date for submissions had latterly been fixed as 1 August 1875, but Tchaikovsky was under the erroneous impression that it was August 1874. He therefore set to work at breakneck speed, feverishly composing *Vakula the Smith* – as the opera was to be called – during the next six weeks at Nizy, and finishing it off and orchestrating it at Ussovo. The date of completion on the autograph score was 21 August 1874.[9] According to the terms of the competition it had to be submitted in a copyist's

[8]RI, Vol. V, pp. 353–4.
[9]RN, p. 106.

hand under a pseudonym, but Tchaikovsky used a pseudonym, 'Ars longa vita brevis', which was well known to be his motto, and which was furthermore written in his own hand. On his return to Moscow he impatiently awaited the result, only to learn that he was a year too soon. He instantly regretted having submitted the work at all, since it would in all probability have been performed anyway, prize or no prize, if he had submitted it instead to the Imperial Opera Committee – or so he thought. And it was unendurable that a whole year should elapse before the result was even known. As for a performance, a delay of a further year or even more would be almost inevitable if his previous experience with the Imperial Opera was anything to go by. He accordingly wrote in October first to the Intendant of the Maryinsky, G. P. Kondratyev,[10] and then to Nápravník,[11] asking whether *Vakula* could be performed regardless of the prize. He soon learned of the extreme displeasure his request had caused the Grand Duke Constantine Nicholayevich, chairman of the committee, and he was flatly turned down.[12] An additional reason given for this rejection was that the rights of the libretto belonged to them and not to him. So his work remained in the competition, with some of the committee already knowing who had written it, contrary to the rules. It should now have lain in limbo, but the overture was performed in November in Moscow by Nicholas Rubinstein. Did Tchaikovsky know that Rubinstein was on the committee of judges of the competition? One can imagine Rubinstein, with his usual *bonhomie*, shrugging the whole thing off in the knowledge that everyone knew who was going to win anyway. Even Rimsky-Korsakov, another of the judges, knew all about it. Tchaikovsky's work did eventually win the prize, so that Rimsky-Korsakov was able to write that 'no harm was done'.[13]

The opera did not finally reach the stage until 28 November/6 December 1876. In spite of Cui's prediction that it was bound to be a success, and his tolerably favourable criticisms, the public did not take to it. It was revised nine years afterwards as *Cherevichki* (The Little Slippers), but notwithstanding fairly considerable insertions and deletions and the substitution of pithy recitative for longer drawn-out *arioso* passages, which made the movement much racier, the original conception was still basically what Tchaikovsky had in mind when he wrote to Jurgenson in 1890: 'So far as the music is concerned, I

[10] No relation of his friend N. D. Kondratyev.
[11] RI, Vol. V, pp. 370–1.
[12] RN, p. 107.
[13] RD, p. 131.

consider it well-nigh my best opera.'[14] A study of the score[15] amply
bears out his opinion of it. It abounds in the most gloriously lyrical
invention, appropriately harmonized in accordance with the dictates
of the Petersburg composers – he was certain when composing it that
at least some of them were sure to be judges in the competition. It is
also full of Russian and Ukrainian folk-like music in the most exquisite
taste, such as the Ukrainian *hopak* (the duet for the Devil and the
witch Solokha in Act I), also used for Vakula's aerial ride on the
Devil's back from Dikanka in the Ukraine to Petersburg; Solokha's
duet with Oksana at the beginning of Act IV; and the dance of the
Zaporozhtsy Cossacks and the Russian dance in Act III, scene 2.
This Russian dance is of the *kazachok* type, deriving not only from
Dargomyzhsky's *Kazachok*, which Tchaikovsky knew well, but from
the second subject of the *lezginka* from Glinka's *Russlan and Ludmilla*
(a *kazachok* and not an 'oriental' dance at all). The opera is placed
fairly well by this; it is the opera of the 'complete Russlanite' which
Tchaikovsky very well knew ought to be approved of by the 'mighty
handful'. The magnificent B major melody in which the Devil evokes
the snowstorm in the first act, of a type Borodin used to such great
effect, stems from the B major chorus to Lel in the first act of *Russlan*;
the F minor chorus of mermaids, complete with Glinka-like triplets,
at the beginning of Act III derives from the charming female choruses
in Acts III and IV of *Russlan*; and the whole-tone scale – used at the
end of Act I, scene 1 – had also been used by Glinka in *Russlan*. But
of these and all the many other examples that could be cited, perhaps
the most interesting is Vakula's superb C minor aria, in which he
laments the frigidity of the engaging but rather cruelly coquettish
Oksana at the end of Act II, scene 1 (Ex. 8(a)), bearing as it does a
close relationship to Ludmilla's aria in Act IV of *Russlan* (Ex. 8(b)).

The Bellini-like triplet accompaniment in the *Russlan* example, and
the Bellini-cum-Verdi type of accompaniment in Tchaikovsky's work
betray the origins of both arias, although the superficial resemblance
of the opening notes should be not taken too greatly into account. All
the same, just as there is hardly a Verdi opera in which this type and
shape of melody is not used, so Tchaikovsky employs it a great deal
elsewhere, for example in the *canzonetta* of the Violin Concerto.
Furthermore Rimsky-Korsakov was certainly evoking a probably
subconscious memory of Tchaikovsky's aria in the Swan Princess's

[14] R J, Vol. II, p. 171.
[15] *Polnoe Sobranie Sochineny*, Vols. 7(a) and 7(b) (Moscow, 1951).

Ex. 8

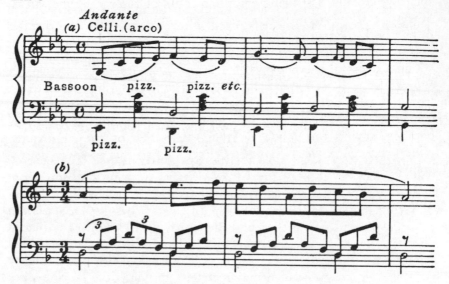

Leitmotiv in his opera *Tsar Saltan* (1900), since the first eight notes, with their concomitant rhythm, are identical, except that Rimsky-Korsakov's is in the major mode. More importantly, Tchaikovsky's delicate instrumentation, derived from Glinka, influenced Rimsky-Korsakov. In *Vakula* the orchestration is transparent, and in fact he was later to write that it was '*even like chamber-music*'. Another reason he gave for its initial failure with the general public was that it was 'over-filled with details ... too musical and not theatrical enough, the harmony too chromatic'.[16] This may have been a valid reason for its failure at the time, but for us today this wealth of superb lyricism, this lack of tawdry theatricality, and the exquisite chromaticism of the harmony must surely be its crowning glories. Here is a Gogol-Ukraine comic opera second only to what Mussorgsky would have achieved had he completed the unfinished *Sorochintsy Fair* before his alcoholism had gone too far, and equal if not superior to Rimsky-Korsakov's *May Night* (1878–9), which is so much indebted to it.

Vakula/Cherevichki, like the Second Symphony, clearly reveals Tchaikovsky's exquisite charm – a facet of his personality testified to by all who knew him, but not sufficiently appreciated by those whose minds are not large enough to allow that a man who was to reveal

[16] RK, Vol. I, p. 467; EO(2), pp. 136–7 (Gerald Abraham's translation).

such hysterically despairing emotions could at the same time, on the other side of the coin, possess not merely superficial but innate charm. In fact both the frustration and the charm were equally a result of his upbringing as a gentleman. But the charm of *Vakula, Swan Lake*, the Violin Concerto, the Serenade for Strings, the Italian Capriccio, the *Scherzo* from the *Manfred* Symphony and countless other works dating from all periods of his life was certainly not merely the tinselly substitute for the real thing that some biographers and film directors, perhaps relying too much on their memories of the unfortunate *Nutcracker* Suite, would have us believe was all this partially warped man was capable of.

5

Increasing subjectiveness (1874–6)

Tchaikovsky was extremely prolific during the twenty-seven months between the completion and production of *Vakula the Smith*. In his feverish activity he was working simultaneously towards a climax in his composition and an emotional nadir, coupled with disgust brought on by an increasing sexual activity which is much more likely to have been auto-erotic in the main rather than actively homosexual, but leading to a profound desire for marriage as a curiously illogical way out of his difficulties. Thus in the autumn of 1876 he was to tell Modest that he was determined to marry;[1] he would break for ever with his 'habits'.[2] Soon afterwards, however, he wrote that he had already broken this resolution three times. But the climacteric was not to be reached until 1877.

Of the less important works composed during this period the group of twelve piano pieces churned out in haste every month for publication in a periodical, and later published under the collective title *The Seasons*, are of negligible value, but in one or two of the songs he does rise above the commonplace, for example in the dramatic 'The Corals' (Op. 28, No. 2) and the sensitive 'Why did I dream of you' (Op. 28, No. 3), composed immediately after he had received the vocal score of Bizet's *Carmen* from Shilovsky in Paris. For lack of a suitable libretto he had no opera in hand at the time (March 1875), so that some good material which might otherwise have been reserved for opera appeared instead in these songs. But the best of the non-orchestral works was the Third String Quartet in E♭ minor, composed in memory of the violinist Ferdinand Laub, whose sudden death had shocked him. This quartet matches and perhaps even surpasses the other two, especially in its superb first movement. The first violin plays a very important role throughout for obvious reasons. Tchaikovsky had already tried his hand at a work for solo violin – the *Sérénade*

[1] RN, p. 132, letter of 19/31 August 1876.
[2] Letter of 10/22 September.

Mélancolique for violin and orchestra dedicated to Leopold Auer, which may well have originated as a sketch for a violin concerto as it followed soon after the Piano Concerto in B♭ minor.

The arguments adduced to disparage the flamboyant Meyerbeerian-Lisztian introductory theme of this justly popular concerto have been myriad, especially as Tchaikovsky made the structural 'blunder' of never allowing the theme to occur again after the introduction, either in the first movement or in the rest of the concerto, thus 'upsetting' the formal balance and producing a 'lopsided' effect. Pages of explication have been written (with diagrams); there has been speculation as to the probability of his having originally intended to bring the theme back later on in the work. But it has also been correctly pointed out that the introductory theme and the second subject of the finale are very similar in type. In addition, both are in D♭ major, and both in three-four time. The one rings up the curtain and the other brings it down, and that surely ought to be a good enough balance for anyone.

Within the boundaries of those two splendidly arresting themes lies a very fine concerto indeed, its delicacy matching the deliberate brashness of the external sections. Tchaikovsky's brilliantly effective use of Ukrainian folk-themes as the principal subjects in both the first and last movements places the concerto within the nationalist orbit. The superbly lyrical and gloriously beautiful slow movement – with its amusingly frivolous scurrying central section based on the French *chansonette* 'Il faut s'amuser, danser et rire' – acts as a crown to the whole work, or, to put it more appropriately, as an apex to the arch whose bases are the extrovert D♭ major themes, with the integral B♭ minor folk-themes half way up on either side; the arch is of course decorated by other themes, modulations and filigree work, but this basic simplification of the structure is in essence the truth of the matter.

Tchaikovsky first played over his concerto, which he had not yet orchestrated, to Nicholas Rubinstein on Christmas Eve, 1874. In a self-pitying letter to Mme von Meck three years later[3] he told her of Rubinstein's destructive criticism. Rubinstein had asserted that the piano part was 'unplayable', that it was so bad that it was hardly worth attempting to revise it, though when he saw how mortified Tchaikovsky was by his remarks he later said that if the concerto were changed to 'suit his requirements' he would play it. This Tchaikovsky refused to do, and his alleged intention of dedicating the concerto to

[3] RK, Vol. I, pp. 172–4.

Rubinstein was revoked.[4] When he completed the orchestral score the following month he dedicated it to Sergei Taneyev, but then scored out this dedication and wrote in 'Hans von Bülow' instead, since that pianist, having already praised and played his music, would no doubt promulgate the concerto much more widely than would be possible for the young, unknown Russian pianist.

Von Bülow was delighted with the dedication and wrote in gratifyingly fulsome terms of the concerto.[5] But in a subsequent letter he rather spoilt the effect of his previous flattery by writing to Tchaikovsky: 'You are one of the five [of my contemporaries] whom I consider have the most marked individuality of our time: the others are Brahms, Raff, Rheinberger and Camille Saint-Saëns.'[6] Tchaikovsky told Mme von Meck that he was very flattered to be numbered in the same company as Brahms, Raff and Saint-Saëns, but the inclusion in the list of Rheinberger 'amazed' him.[7]

Von Bülow gave the first performance of the concerto while on a tour of the United States of America, on 13/25 October in Boston, and immediately afterwards sent news of its success to Tchaikovsky in a cablegram thought to be the first ever to be sent between Boston and Moscow. The Russian première followed in Petersburg, and in Moscow it was brilliantly performed by Taneyev. This Moscow performance was conducted by none other than Nicholas Rubinstein himself, who soon realized the error of his first judgment. Tchaikovsky had told him that he would 'not alter a single note',[8] and in the first edition (1875) he was as good as his word, but he subsequently allowed alterations to be made in the layout of the piano part by Edward Dannreuther for a performance in London in 1876 and he incorporated practically all these changes in the second edition (1879). A third edition was published in 1889 in the preparation of which he consulted his friend the pianist Alexander Siloti. As James Friskin has pointed out,[9] it was in this last edition that the piano chords accompanying the opening theme were written to cover the *whole* range of the instrument. Thus the glittering effect so well known to us today was not Tchaikovsky's original intention or, if it was, he did not adequately achieve it. In fact many of the alterations by Dannreuther were in the

---

[4] According to Kashkin, RB(1), p. 95 *et seq.*
[5] RM, pp. 197–8.
[6] *ibid.*, p. 198.
[7] RI, Vol. VIII, p. 71.
[8] See note 3 above.
[9] ET.

rather ham-handed original piano part, which is after all what Rubinstein had been chiefly complaining of.

Tchaikovsky did not go abroad in the summer of 1875, but divided his holiday as usual between Ussovo, Nizy and not Kamenka this time but nearby Verbovka which also belonged to the Davydovs. He devoted his time to writing his Third Symphony in D major. A year before he had revised his First Symphony in the light of his experience in writing the Second,[10] but he still remained dissatisfied with his symphonic techniques, particularly in the all-important first movement. He had so far achieved development by means of characteristic decoration and frequent repetition at different pitches and with different instrumentation, with here and there the use of contrapuntal and canonic devices, but there had been nothing in the way of developmental evolution. Clearly in this symphony the introductory funeral march is meant to contain the seeds of the first subject of the *Allegro brillante*, but except for the dotted-note rhythm there is little common to them either in mood or in actual melodic material. How much better both Borodin and Balakirev achieved this kind of thing in their first symphonies! The working of the material in the first movement shows that Tchaikovsky, in order to improve his symphonic techniques, has gone to the Schumann of the symphonies. It is curious that he should have done this, since Schumann's symphonies have little to offer a composer wishing to learn how to evolve his material rather than to decorate it.

He felt that up till then his first-movement themes had had too much character to be capable of this kind of development, hence the first subject of the movement is plain, based on simple arpeggio and scale passages. Significantly, less than three years later he was to write to Mme von Meck: 'Countless new and pleasing melodic combinations can still be derived from [the common chord]... Melodies by Beethoven, Weber, Mendelssohn and above all Wagner are frequently constructed upon the notes of the triad, and a talented musician can always invent a new and beautiful melody derived from the notes of a fanfare.' He maintained that 'it is only talent that counts ... and enables beautiful music to be created out of *nothing*'.[11]

Unfortunately, even if it is 'created out of nothing', the first movement of this symphony is no masterpiece. The feeble four-square development of the first subject, the equally four-square nature of the

[10] The *original* version of the Second Symphony, of course.
[11] RK, Vol. I, pp. 375–6.

second subject, a theme derived from Schumann – for instance, the second subject of the first movement of the Third Symphony – but twisted round by means of weak repetitions to seem to bear a faint resemblance to Russian folk-song, these do not add up to successful exploitation of the medium. Most of the finale is trite in the extreme. But some of the development passages both here and in the first movement reveal that the same hand is at work as in the B♭ minor Piano Concerto, and there is still some evidence of the influence of Balakirev, whose Czech Overture, later revised as the Symphonic Poem *In Bohemia*, Tchaikovsky had heard at its first performance in Moscow in 1867. Compare the following passage from Balakirev's Czech Overture (Ex. 9(a)) with a passage from the finale of Tchaikovsky's Third Symphony (Ex. 9(b)).

Like Schumann's Third Symphony, Tchaikovsky's has five movements, but the intermezzo, instead of being a solemn tone-picture preceding the finale as in Schumann's, is here an *alla tedesca* between the opening and slow movements. This valse is derived from Glinka's *Valse-Fantasie*, originally a piano piece (later orchestrated by the composer) which in turn had its origins in Weber's *Invitation to the Dance*, but despite Tchaikovsky's title there is nothing more German about the movement than this derivation. Compare the opening of the main theme of the Glinka *Valse-Fantasie* (Ex. 10(a)) with the beginning of the second half of Tchaikovsky's Valse (Ex. 10(b)). The chattering triplets of the trio, first on the wind and then on the strings, are a typical mannerism which he was to use to greater effect in later works such as the march from the Sixth Symphony, and the lugubrious bassoon solo with its tonic-subdominant harmonization[12] was clearly in his mind when he composed the main theme of the first movement of his Fifth Symphony, where the similar march-like material is much more rhythmically varied and alive. But the *Scherzo*, in B minor, which we know he studied again before composing the unsurpassed *Scherzo* of the *Manfred* Symphony,[13] is a movement which is not the mere precursor of that or any other later music of the composer, but an exquisite gem in its own right that includes the really charming use of the whole-tone scale. Its march-like trio is based on music rescued from his 1872 occasional cantata. In both the scherzo and the trio the instrumentation is entirely individual. We have noted how Tchaikovsky's treatment of the orchestra in these years was much admired

[12] Eulenburg miniature score, p. 92.
[13] EU, p. 118.

Ex. 9

Ex. 10

by Rimsky-Korsakov. It is curious that Cui, who praised the first three movements, should have remarked in his review of the symphony that the scherzo was interesting only as sound, 'almost without musical content';[14] for Rimsky-Korsakov was later to be accused of exactly the same fault. The elusive nature of the music here is one of its boldest and most original qualities, and, coming as it did from a composer well known for his lavishly lyrical themes, its meaning totally eluded Cui. Not so Balakirev, who considered it one of Tchaikovsky's best movements. In the symphony as a whole Tchaikovsky failed to achieve the technical advances he so greatly desired; it was only much later that he was fully able to carry out what he undoubtedly adumbrates here. But at the time he did think that 'it's a technical step forward', as he wrote to Rimsky-Korsakov.[15]

In response to a commission from the directorate of the Imperial Theatres in Moscow, Tchaikovsky had started work on a new ballet, *Swan Lake*, incorporating some earlier music, including what he had

[14]RN, p. 124.
[15]RI, Vol. V, p. 417, letter of 12/24 November 1875.

composed three years before for the Davydov children. It was not finished until April the following year, and the first performance, a rather shoddy, ill-prepared affair, did not take place until February 1877. The score was clearly of too substantial a nature for the ballet-going public of the day, who were used to a much more frivolous 'accompaniment' to the dancing, just as the amateurish conductor found the music too difficult technically, accustomed as he was to playing music by Adam, Minkus, Gerber, Pugni and their like.

In *Swan Lake* Tchaikovsky was not influenced at all by Delibes, the only composer of the day comparable to him in the writing of ballet music. Delibes's ballet *Sylvia*, which he was later to rave about, considering it to be 'a thousand times finer' than *The Ring*, did not receive its first performance until three months after the completion of *Swan Lake*. Moreover he did not get to know Delibes's earlier ballet *Coppélia* until 1878. Accordingly it is clear that his genius for ballet music was original but was not appreciated at the time of the early performances of *Swan Lake* because of the appalling production. In addition, owing to their not being 'sufficiently danceable', several numbers were cut altogether and other more familiar music (by Pugni) was substituted. It was only with the choreography of Petipa and Ivanov in the production two years after Tchaikovsky's death that the classic *Swan Lake* we know today was created.

In the last months of 1875 Tchaikovsky was in very high spirits. His Piano Concerto was acclaimed in the U.S.A. and in Russia, and the first performance of his Third Symphony in Moscow was gratifyingly successful. He became intimate with Saint-Saëns, who was on a visit to Moscow. Both being passionately fond of ballet, they staged an impromptu one called *Pygmalion and Galatea*, Tchaikovsky as Pygmalion bringing to life the stony Galatea in the person of Saint-Saëns, to appropriate piano music provided equally off the cuff by Nicholas Rubinstein. Désirée Artôt-Padilla had appeared as Valentine in *Les Huguenots*, Tchaikovsky informed Anatol, on 10/22 December, but the old flame had been extinguished long ago. She was 'shockingly fat' and had 'almost lost her voice', but her 'talent still makes an impression'.[16] He now received official notification that he had won the prize for *Vakula* and that it would be performed at the Maryinsky the following season, but more satisfactory even than this was the knowledge that Modest, about whom he had been very worried, had at last found a suitable job as tutor to a deaf and dumb boy, Nicholas

[16] *ibid.*, p. 424.

(Kolya) Konradi. Kolya's father wanted Modest to go to Lyons for a year to study a method of teaching deaf-mutes there. Tchaikovsky accompanied his brother as far as Paris, which they reached by way of Berlin and Geneva. In Paris they went to a performance of *Carmen*. Tchaikovsky's 'unhealthy passion' for this opera – as Modest called it[17] – had only been increased by the tragic death of the composer soon after its lukewarm initial reception. He was electrified by Célestine Galli-Marié's interpretation of the title-role, combining as it did uncontrolled passion and an element of mystic fatalism. This whole atmosphere, as it was subjectively perceived and subconsciously brooded upon by the hypersensitive Russian composer, was to enter into his own compositions more and more. Those feelings, hitherto relatively latent in him, were almost brutally stimulated by *Carmen*.

He was looking for a suitable opera subject, and now clearly the more like *Carmen* it was the better. Shilovsky's brother Constantine had written a libretto on the subject of *Ephraim*. He was, however, much more attracted to *Francesca da Rimini*, but in the end he rejected a ready-made libretto on the subject by Zvantsev,[18] since the librettist wanted his work to be treated in the Wagnerian style. On going to the original source of the story, Canto V of Dante's *Inferno*, he decided to write not an opera but an orchestral piece, which he sketched out the following summer. He was again in western Europe, having been ordered to Vichy for the cure after an illness in Russia during the spring. He visited Modest in Lyons, going on by way of Paris to Bayreuth to report for *Russkiye Vyedomosti* the first complete performance of *The Ring* in August.

Tchaikovsky's reports give a vivid picture of these first exciting days at Bayreuth. He was graciously received by Liszt, but Wagner was 'receiving no one'. His critiques on *The Ring* were on the whole fair, but he privately expressed his true opinions in letters to Modest. Of *Das Rheingold*: 'As music it is incredible nonsense', although it had its 'moments of extraordinary beauty' (letter of 2/14 August); while after *Götterdämmerung*: 'I felt as though I'd been set free from prison. It may be that the *Nibelungen* is a great masterpiece, but there surely was never anything more boring or long-winded than this interminable thing' (letter of 8/20 August).[19] By the time Tchaikovsky wrote this last tirade he was already in Vienna on his way home. He was

[17] RH, Vol. I, p. 479.
[18] RN, p. 125.
[19] *ibid*, p. 131; RL, pp. 110–12.

becoming increasingly intoxicated by the idea of marriage, as his letters to Modest and Anatol show, but he promised not to take the plunge precipitately.

After the composition of the *Slavonic March* – originally called *Serbo-Russian March* – written in a fit of patriotism during the Serbo-Turkish war for a concert in aid of wounded Serb soldiers, he got to work in earnest on *Francesca da Rimini*, completing the full score on 5/17 November. The following month, immediately after the first performance of *Vakula the Smith*, he wrote the *Variations on a Rococo Theme* for cello and orchestra.

Two more different works could hardly have been conceived contemporaneously. *Francesca* was considered by the Petersburg composers to be the summit of Tchaikovsky's achievement up till then, and Laroche[20] and other more eclectic critics were equally attracted to it. The greater subjectiveness of Tchaikovsky's music is everywhere apparent, not least in the beautiful central themes associated with Francesca herself, particularly the second upward-surging melody over a pedal; this seems to depict Francesca's uncontrollable urge for illicit love, with which Tchaikovsky was so well able to identify himself. In spite of this new subjectiveness here and elsewhere, he was still close enough to the folk/Glinka/Balakirev influence for it to have been possible for the 'mighty handful' to identify themselves with the music. Tchaikovsky's recent attendance at the *Ring* cycle also had an influence upon *Francesca*, as Cui pointed out later. He was an impressionable person, and it was perhaps a tribute to the power of Wagner's music that, despite all conscious effort, it should have borne fruit in this way. But it was also a tribute to the strength of Tchaikovsky's personality by this stage in his career that any influence of *The Ring* – mainly in the *Allegro vivo* sections – was so incorporated into his own personal style that hardly a single bar could be mistaken for the music of Wagner. Far more important than any actual physical resemblances in the music or orchestration is the time-scale in which the work is conceived. For example, it is not without importance that after a long introduction of sixty-six bars the *Allegro vivo* whirlwind has been in progress for a further seventy-one bars before the main theme is first heard in its entirety. Tchaikovsky had not previously attempted to think in terms of such a broad time-scale, to paint on such a large canvas.

On the other hand any influence on the much smaller-scale *Variations*

---

[20]RC, Vol. II, pp. 43–8.

on a Rococo Theme, written for his colleague Fitzenhagen, is the influence not of Wagner but of Mozart. Tchaikovsky always worshipped the music of Mozart, seeing it, through rose-tinted spectacles, as the perfection of a past age in comparison with which his contemporary era was debased and vulgar. In the court scene in *Vakula* he had already written a neo-rococo minuet, and he was periodically to indulge himself further in this way, as, for example, in the Orchestral Suites – the Fourth is an arrangement of actual music by Mozart – and *The Queen of Spades*.

Not that the *Rococo Variations* are in the least like Mozart, just as Brahms's *Variations on a Theme by Haydn*, written a decade earlier, are not in the least like Haydn. In any case Brahms's theme was not by Haydn, though he did not know this, nor does the eighteenth-century sized orchestra for which he, like Tchaikovsky, wrote his variations sound in the least like an eighteenth-century orchestra. The same is true of Tchaikovsky, for whom it was enough that the charm and delicacy of the eighteenth century should be matched, together with the rather four-square 'classical' shape of the original theme.[21] But whereas Brahms's variations were in the direct line of the development of his symphonic thought, this is much truer of Tchaikovsky's *Francesca* than of his *Rococo Variations*, which were on the contrary in a world of happy make-believe where the frustrations and terrors of present existence could be forgotten for a time in the contemplation of the past.

However, it was not in the writing of such works that he was to find an anodyne in the next few years, but in his correspondence with Mme von Meck, started, curiously enough, within a day or two of the composition of the *Rococo Variations* in December.

---

[21] Unlike Brahms's theme, the St Antony Choral, whose chief attraction is its irregular shape.

6

The climacteric (1876–7)

The recently widowed Nadezhda Filaretovna von Meck first became acquainted with Tchaikovsky's music through *The Tempest*, probably brought to her notice by Nicholas Rubinstein, who suggested that she might commission a work from him since he was in financial difficulties. This cultured, much-travelled, enormously wealthy lady, in spite of her eleven surviving children, seven of whom still lived with her, was to find in music an emotional release which she had never achieved in her domestic relationship with her husband. (At first she had tried to achieve this emotional release in another way, since her husband died of a heart attack on learning of her infidelity.) It was owing to her business acumen as much as to her husband's engineering skill that the railways which brought them fortune had been built, and it was she who, as a result of emotional frustration, tended to domineer her family. After her husband's death, with the exception of her immediate family and Nicholas Rubinstein, who kept her in touch with the musical world, the severely shocked Mme von Meck saw practically no one and shut herself away from the world. She continued to travel widely, but only in her own special trains and coaches, surrounded by her family. Included in the family circle was always a musician who could play to her, since she disliked going to public concerts because of the pathological aversion to humanity in the mass caused by her state of shock.

The violinist Joseph Kotek, a former pupil of Tchaikovsky's who adored his music, was appointed to her staff soon after her husband died in 1876 and was not slow to sing the praises of Tchaikovsky to his employer. The result of his and Rubinstein's recommendations was a generous commission to arrange for violin and piano some of his smaller pieces. Tchaikovsky was quick to comply, and thus started their freakish pen-relationship in which each seemed to bare the soul before the other, Nadezhda von Meck sincerely and increasingly gushingly, Tchaikovsky less sincerely to begin with, but much more so before the lapse of many months. Each was determined never to meet the other in the flesh. 'The more fascinating you are to me, the more afraid I am of making your acquaintance,' she declared. Tchaikovsky replied that this 'misanthropy' or rather fear of dis-illusionment which 'frequently follows upon all intimacy' was a further link between them. It was with his music rather than with him that she was in love, and she answered that for her the 'ideal man is a musician'. She commissioned him to arrange for her a funeral march from a passage in *The Oprichnik* which she told him 'drives me to distraction'.[1] The fee offered was hardly less lavish than her praise.

Meanwhile Tchaikovsky was becoming more and more dissatisfied with his work at the Conservatoire, which was interfering with composition. For immediately after *Francesca* and the *Rococo Variations* followed work on his next symphony, the fourth. In this symphony he was trying to achieve something new, although he did not quite know himself what it was. The work caused him some difficulty and he became depressed and overwrought. The idea of the influence of 'Fate' in life had again become an obsession with him since he had heard *Carmen* a year earlier, and this idea is central in the Fourth Symphony. It is even possible that the 'Fate' motive itself from the introduction to the opera, with its descending sequences, influenced the first subject of the first movement in the tortured valse derived from a not dissimilar musical shape. And this puts the symphony firmly in its place, for it is an 'operatic' symphony. He had written the previous summer that Wagner's *Ring* was more symphonic than operatic. Now he was attempting a symphony that was no less theatrical than it was symphonic, unlike the opera he was shortly to embark upon, *Eugene Onegin*, which he later averred was 'not theatrical enough'. Indeed he wrote to Taneyev in this connection that he could 'spit on all stage effect', but when he wrote this he was thinking of the opera, not the symphony.

Then, towards the end of April, when the nervous strain was becoming serious, he received a love letter out of the blue from one Antonina Ivanovna Milyukova. She alleged that she had met him some time earlier at the Conservatoire, but otherwise she had been content up till then to admire and love him from afar. He occasionally received letters of this sort and had no recollection of their meeting. He told Kashkin afterwards that he ignored this letter and soon forgot about it.[2] To avoid confusion in the narration of the unfolding of interwoven

[1] RK, Vol. I, pp. 3–9.
[2] RB(2), p. 118.

events and creative work in the next few months it will be necessary to keep to their strict chronological order. On 30 April/12 May[3] Mme von Meck commissioned Tchaikovsky to write a piece called *The Reproach* for violin and piano in which must be heard the yearning of unhappiness, the surrender to despair ... and even death, 'for music can give solace which cannot be found in real life'. On the next day, however, he replied that he was unable to fulfil her commission as he was working very hard on his symphony, which 'I'd very much like to dedicate to you'. He was in an 'irritated' frame of mind, so that the symphony was making only 'slow progress'. He told her he was in financial difficulties and very deprecatingly asked her for the loan of 3,000 roubles.[4] She immediately complied with his request, begging him not to think of paying it back and accepting the dedication of the symphony. Tchaikovsky was overwhelmed with gratitude in his next letter (3/15 May),[5] by which time the short score of the first three movements of the symphony had been completed.

Within the next few days he received two more letters from Antonina Milyukova, in which she asked him not to be so cruel as to refuse to meet her at least once and threatened suicide. Tchaikovsky made inquiries about her from the pianist E. L. Langer and received a reply that was unfavourable towards this 'unsophisticated' character.[6] On 8/20 May he wrote to Klimenko of his desire for 'marriage or some other permanent union'.[7] On 13/25 May Elizaveta Lavrovskaya suggested Pushkin's *Eugene Onegin* as an opera text. At first cool towards the idea, he changed his mind on the next day, bought a copy of Pushkin – Vol. I of the 1838 edition – and worked all the following night on a scenario which was roughed out by the morning. For the week-end 15–17/27–29 May he went to the Shilovsky house at Glebovo in order to work at the scenario with Constantine (Vladimir's brother).[8]

Tchaikovsky's thoughts once again returned to Antonina. He later told Mme von Meck[9] that he decided to answer her letter because it was so 'warmly and sincerely written', although in previous cases he had always avoided doing this, and he 'accepted her invitation to visit her', which he did on 20 May/1 June. He told her that he could never

[3] RK, Vol. I, pp. 12–13.
[4] *ibid.*, pp. 14–16.
[5] *ibid.*, pp. 18–20.
[6] RB(2), p. 109.
[7] RN, p. 146.
[8] RL, pp. 120–1.
[9] Letter of 3/15 July 1877, RK, Vol. I, pp. 25–8.

love her, but only be grateful for her love and sympathetic towards her. But immersed as he was in his scenario of *Eugene Onegin* and obsessed with the pathos of Tatyana's unrequited love and Onegin's brusque rebuttal, he reflected that he had 'acted thoughtlessly'. His visit to her may well have raised her hopes, and could he now heartlessly drop her, suicidally inclined as she was? He visited her again a day or two later and finally, refusing to behave as unfeelingly as Onegin (or so he alleged later to Kashkin),[10] he took the fatally foolish step of proposing marriage to Antonina, who accepted him with alacrity. 'I'm marrying a girl who is no longer very young' – she was twenty-eight – 'but she is eminently suitable', he wrote to Anatol a month later.[11] (Meanwhile he told nobody.) He imagined that this unsophisticated girl would suit him as well as his father's third wife suited the old man, who was in his seventies when he married her. Tchaikovsky explained carefully to the 'no longer young' Antonina that their marriage must be Platonic, and had she really loved his music – he later discovered that she was totally unacquainted with it – and had she really been devoted to him it might have worked out. As it was, she was not only empty headed but suffered from *folie de grandeur*. The truth of the matter was that, although she agreed to the marriage on his terms, she never for a moment doubted that she would be able to bring him round, that it was only a matter of time before he would surely succumb to her feminine charms, in spite of his true nature, at which he had certainly hinted, if nothing more.

During this time he completed the short score of the finale of the Fourth Symphony, which reveals, in a much more unbridled fashion than *Onegin* was to do, the tempestuous emotions which had been unleashed in him during these fatal days towards the end of May. With the main work of the symphony behind him, as soon as he arrived again at Glebovo on 29 May/11 June for the first part of his summer holiday, he was able to concentrate in earnest on *Eugene Onegin*, finishing the whole of the second scene of Act I (composed first) by 6/18 June.[12] Since it includes Tatyana's letter, of central importance in the whole opera, the speed with which its composition was achieved was remarkable, even if he had made sketches of it before arriving at Glebovo. With his extraordinary engagement still a secret between himself and his fiancée, he retired mentally into the

---

[10] See RB(2) and EO(4), pp. 228–9.
[11] RN, p. 147.
[12] RH, Vol. II, p. 204.

fairy-tale world of Tatyana's story, identifying himself with her to an exceptional degree and writing music of a lyrical charm and an intensely felt quality of expression which is never overdone. Even Onegin, whose character and behaviour he found repellent, is treated in a remarkably restrained manner. There is no sign anywhere in the whole opera of the near hysteria which is to be found in certain passages of the symphony. On 15/27 June he was able to write to Anatol that 'the whole of the first act in three scenes is now ready, I have today begun the second... Criticize *Eugene Onegin* if you like, but I'm writing the music with enormous pleasure'.[13] But by 23 June/5 July, with two-thirds of the opera already sketched out, he had to come out of this cloud cuckoo-land and, for the first time, wrote to his family to tell them about his forthcoming marriage. It was not, however, to the homosexual Modest, nor to his beloved sister Sasha that he wrote. He sent them letters only on the day before his wedding, so that he would already be married before they knew anything about it. It was his eighty-two year old father that he really wanted to tell, and he enclosed a note to him in an explanatory letter to Anatol. He told Anatol not to worry, and that he had not intended to write to him until after the wedding, but that it would be wrong to marry 'without Father's blessing'. Both Anatol and his father were enjoined to strict secrecy. In his reply his father duly blessed Peter and expressed his delight emphatically.[14]

Towards the end of June Tchaikovsky left Glebovo, excusing his abrupt departure by telling Shilovsky that he must visit his old father in St Petersburg. But he went instead to Moscow to make preparations for his wedding. With only three days to go he at last plucked up enough courage to write a long letter to Mme von Meck, giving her the details already related.[15] One of the reasons he gave for his decision to marry was that his father always wished it, and that Fate had decreed his meeting with the girl. 'No man can escape his destiny,' he wrote. 'What is to be, will be.' This typically Russian fatalism was brought to a head in Tchaikovsky's case, as we have seen, by his morbidly intense reaction to *Carmen*, and by his identification of Tatyana's feelings with those of his betrothed. He was living out his own life as if it were a favourite opera or poem; fiction was being mixed up with fact. But he made quite sure of one thing: that Nadezhda

[13]RL, p. 123. In a letter of 21 May/2 June Anatol had expressed doubts about the suitability of the subject (*ibid.*, p. 577).
[14]RN, p. 148.
[15]See note 9 above.

von Meck knew that he did not love Antonina. Her tactful reply to him contained nothing in the way of reproof, only sympathy.[16] Yet her true feelings were very different, as she wrote to him some two years later. The thought that 'that woman' was near to him had been 'bitter and unbearable'. She rejoiced when he was unhappy with her. She hated Antonina 'because she didn't make you happy, but I'd have hated her a hundred times more if you had found happiness with her'. Antonina had robbed her of what should have been hers alone, because she herself loved him 'more than any one else' and put a 'higher value' upon him 'than upon anything else in the world'.[17] All this was written after she had been playing over the recently published piano transcription of the Fourth Symphony, dedicated to her not by name but, by her wish, 'to my best friend', and her uncontrolled enthusiasm for the symphony led her to tell him in September 1879 what her true feelings had been in July 1877. But they were successfully concealed at the time.

After the marriage ceremony on 6/18 July the pair went to Petersburg to visit Tchaikovsky's father, returning on 14/26 to Moscow, where Tchaikovsky received a letter of congratulations from Sasha.[18] After the obligatory visit to his mother-in-law he confessed that he detested not only her but the whole of his wife's narrow-minded bickering family. His only confidant was Kotek, except for Mme von Meck, to whom he poured out his soul in a letter from Kiev on 28 July/9 August.[19] He had fled to Kiev on his way to his sister's at Kamenka, telling his wife – and Mme von Meck, from whom he had obtained 1,000 roubles for the purpose – that he had to take the cure in the Caucasus. So for the month of August he was reprieved and his shuddering horror at the thought of being merely in the same room as his wife was temporarily forgotten. He told Mme von Meck that when he left Moscow he felt as though he had 'woken up from a frightening, painful nightmare'. Through no fault of hers his wife was 'repellent' to him, and composition was impossible in her proximity. His future stretched out before him as a 'vegetable existence'.

But the friendly, intimate Davydov household soon calmed his agitated nerves and he started to orchestrate the symphony, informing Mme von Meck on 12/24 August that although the orchestration of the first movement would be difficult because of its complexity and

[16] RK, Vol. I, pp. 28–9.
[17] RK, Vol. II, pp. 212–13.
[18] RN, p. 149.
[19] RK, Vol. I, pp. 32–5.

length, the other three movements would be simple and fun to orchestrate. 'The scherzo [pizzicato] consists of a new instrumental effect of which I have great hopes.'[20] On 27 August/8 September, before this was finished, he started to complete the short score of *Eugene Onegin*. Pushkin himself had sometimes visited Kamenka and its atmosphere was perfect. But he found the end difficult. He was not sure whether Tatyana and Onegin should run off together, which old Alexandra Davydova, his sister's mother-in-law (who had met Pushkin on his visits to her home), told him would be sacrilegious, or whether to give them a passionate love duet before Tatyana dismisses her now passionately devoted – but firmly denied – lover. The definitive version, closest of all to Pushkin, was not written until later. Meanwhile he finished orchestrating the first scene on 30 August/11 September. He wrote that the lack of stage effects in the opera would tell against its popularity. But despite this lack, 'it is written sincerely, and on this sincerity I rest all my hopes'.[21] He was determined to fight his feeling of alienation towards his wife and think of her good qualities, which 'she indubitably possesses'.

The term at the Conservatoire was due to start on 12/24 September, and he would again have to face, day after day, night after night, a wife who had already tried to raise his ardour by boasting of imaginary generals, nephews of famous bankers, well-known artists, not to mention members of the Imperial family itself, who had been smitten with desire for her. But he told Anatol, 'she doesn't frighten me, she's simply a nuisance'. He found the flat she had prepared for them while he was away comfortable, put a brave face on things and introduced his wife to his friends and colleagues at a supper given by Jurgenson. Kashkin met her on this occasion, and commented that he tended to finish his wife's sentences for her, fearing that she might commit some *faux-pas*, trivial though the conversation was.[22]

'Death is indeed the greatest of blessings and I pray for it with all my soul,' he wrote to Mme von Meck.[23] In spite of his words to Anatol, living with his wife did terrify him, and unable to stand the strain any longer (in the middle of September) he decided to commit suicide, but in such a way as to disguise it as accidental death. He found a lonely spot by the Moskva river and waded 'almost up to the waist' in the icy waters, in the hope that pneumonia would result. In

[20] *ibid.*, pp. 40–1.
[21] *ibid.*, pp. 44–5.
[22] RB(2), pp. 110–11.
[23] RK, Vol. I, p. 45.

the end he was forced to return to Antonina none the worse for his ducking, telling her that he had been fishing and had fallen in accidentally.[24] Obviously this half-hearted attempt at suicide was a mere excuse to bring his intolerable life with her to an end. He was able to excuse to himself his impending abrupt desertion of his wife by the subconscious thought that suicide was preferable to living with her – just as she had appeared to think four months before that suicide would be preferable to not living with him.

He telegraphed to Anatol, asking him to send him a wire in Nápravník's name summoning him urgently to Petersburg.[25] He was in a state of complete mental and physical collapse on arrival there. Anatol immediately rushed him to a hotel, where he had a frightening nervous breakdown, followed by a coma that lasted forty-eight hours. The mental specialist who attended him was of the opinion that only a complete change would save his reason. Further contact with his wife would have to be avoided at all costs. Anatol went to Moscow and, accompanied by Nicholas Rubinstein, broke the news to Antonina, who gave them tea and calmly stated that for her husband's sake she would 'endure anything'. To Anatol's astonishment, after Rubinstein had left, she remarked: 'Well now, I never expected I'd have Rubinstein drinking tea with me today.'[26] (Perhaps she even made a mental note to add him to the list of her admirers.) Anatol was horrified at her remark, but it was not prompted so much by stupidity, frivolity or even shallowness of character as by a mental disorder of which these were only symptoms. A hysterical outburst would have been far more natural in the circumstances than this terrifying *sang-froid*. Antonina was to spend the last two decades or so of her life in a mental hospital,[27] but not before she had caused a great deal of distress to her rather less mentally sick husband. Unfortunately nobody at the time, preoccupied as they were with his mental disorder, noticed the ominous signs of hers. That two such disorientated people, whose sexual inversion on the one hand and sexual obsession on the other were symptoms of much deeper neuroses, should have married was a maliciously capricious trick of fate.

[24] RB(2), p. 125.
[25] RN, p. 152.
[26] RB(2), pp. 112–13.
[27] She died in 1917.

7

Aftermath of marriage (1877–8)

At the beginning of October, having written to Modest: 'I'm at last coming to myself and returning to life,'[1] Tchaikovsky set off for western Europe with Anatol. They went first to Clarens in Switzerland, where they stayed for a month, Tchaikovsky finishing the orchestration of the first act of *Onegin*. He wrote to Mme von Meck about his breakdown and again asked her for money, since he had only enough for a few weeks' stay. Meanwhile he received news from Rubinstein that he would be paid his full salary for the session at the Conservatoire and given a sabbatical year. Furthermore he had been invited to become Russian delegate to the Paris Exhibition of 1878, a salaried post. He was not sure that this was the sort of position he would fulfil satisfactorily, but he initially accepted. Shortly afterwards he received a letter from Mme von Meck, who had just returned to Moscow from Italy, whence she had already promised him enough money to allow him to stay abroad for several months. In this letter she informed him of her intention to settle upon him an annuity of 6,000 roubles to free him once and for all from financial difficulties and to allow him to devote all his time to composition. In his letter of gratitude (25 October/6 November) he wrote that 'henceforth every note that emanates from my pen shall be dedicated to you'.[2] When, late in December, he received from the Ministry of Finance the official appointment as Russian delegate to the Paris Exhibition at a thousand francs a month he refused the offer, much to the disgust of Rubinstein, who was particularly piqued that Tchaikovsky had refused the delegateship which he himself had been instrumental in obtaining for him, and which would bring fame both to the composer and to the Moscow Conservatoire – still only a junior sister of its Petersburg counterpart. Instead he was idly living on the gratuities of a rich woman. Rubinstein

[1] RN, p. 153 *et seq.*
[2] The Tchaikovsky-von Meck correspondence concerned with the above is to be found in RK, Vol. I, pp. 47–60.

feared that it would be bad for Tchaikovsky's character and make him 'slothful'; Tchaikovsky was furious with Rubinstein for failing to understand that the freedom thus gained was being put to the best possible use – composition.[3]

He had moved on from Switzerland to Italy, first accompanying Anatol to Vienna on his way back to Russia. Anatol had been asked by his distressed sister and her husband to call at Kamenka and take Antonina home to her mother in Moscow. Sasha had been sorry for her sister-in-law and had invited her to Kamenka from Odessa, where she had originally been established. Sasha even tried to bring the couple together again, and her well-meant interference resulted in some incoherent letters from Antonina to Tchaikovsky. Sasha grew to realize her sister-in-law's true nature, but by this time she was enjoying her stay at Kamenka so much that she refused to consider leaving. Hence Sasha's *cri de cœur* to Anatol to remove her.

It was at this crucial juncture in his career that the correspondence with Nadezhda von Meck was of supreme importance to Tchaikovsky. Her part as confidante was a vital factor in helping him to regain some sort of mental equilibrium, and she rejoiced in her by no means passive role. 'She [Antonina] won't suffer in the least from the separation,' wrote the older woman. 'Don't be upset if you're told that she is in tears . . . Be assured she only does it for show.'[4] (Tchaikovsky had been told of her continual weeping at Kamenka.) The following remark from Mme von Meck was typical: 'I'm waiting impatiently for your new music.' She was afraid he might lose the urge to compose. Tchaikovsky very much wanted to finish the orchestration of the work to be dedicated to his benefactress, but he had left the unfinished score in Russia and its arrival was delayed owing to confusion in the post. However, the scoring was finished on 26 December 1877/7 January 1878, and less than four weeks later *Onegin*, too, was completed.

In spite of his usual reluctance to commit himself to a definite programme in words, he did sketch one out for the Fourth Symphony – 'their' symphony – for Mme von Meck.[5] The 'Fate' motive at the beginning was meant to be the 'germ of the whole symphony'. He likened it to 'the sword of Damocles' that 'hangs over our heads'. The main theme describes feelings of 'depression and hopelessness'. The second group, besides expressing a 'dream world' that was an 'escape

[3]RL, pp. 142–3.
[4]RK, Vol. I, pp. 76–7.
[5]*ibid.*, letter of 17 February/1 March 1878 (pp. 216–20).

from reality', displays the operatic facet that was becoming rooted in Tchaikovsky's symphonic style: there is a change of tempo which heightens the contrast between the harsh tortured dotted-note reality of the first subject and the wispy sylph-like dotted-note dreamland of the second – for there is that connection between the two. All the forms of the subjects, including the opening fanfare, contend violently in the development. In the coda the opening fanfare recurs and the movement closes with the first subject in the form of a horrifying march, *molto più mosso*. Altogether this was Tchaikovsky's most successful sonata movement so far.

Unfortunately the dragging-in by the short hairs of the 'Fate' motive in the festive finale (an idea based on the story of the fateful death of Carmen in the middle of the bull-fighting festivities) is not enough to make this introductory material the 'germ of the whole symphony', and there is no connection with the two middle movements. Tchaikovsky did not achieve success in this type of cyclic form until his Fifth Symphony (1888), in which a solution is found to all the problems left unsolved and in abeyance for a decade. The folk-song 'In the fields there stood a birch tree' is adapted as the second subject of the finale. Unlike the folk-songs used in the Second Symphony and elsewhere this song, like the 'Fate' motive itself later on, is dragged in most inappropriately, squared off with two extra beats and ruined in the process.

The disappointing finale, composed at the time of his proposal of marriage to Antonina, is preceded by the well-known *pizzicato Scherzo* and folk-like wind and brass trio, in which, according to the composer, one may 'suddenly call to mind a scene of some peasants on a carousal, and a street song. Then, somewhere a long way off, a military procession passes by.' We need not bother overmuch about the possible prototypes of the *Scherzo* – a movement from Delibes's *Sylvia* and balalaika-like choruses in Glinka. In spite of any superficial derivations, it is an original stroke of genius. And the symphony as a whole was 'a technical step forward in my development', as he wrote to Mme von Meck.[6]

But the most important step forward was in emotional involvement. All the frustrations of his endemic homosexuality and bottled-up emotions, further engendered rather than released by the fiasco of his marriage, are let loose in this symphony – the first and perhaps least important work in a line of masterpieces or near-masterpieces in this vein which included the *Manfred* Symphony and the last

[6] *ibid.*, p. 142.

two symphonies, the Symphonic Ballad *The Voyevoda* and *The Queen of Spades*, to name a few. Nevertheless the conflict between escapism and reality is not entirely convincing and, for all the great contrasts and the emotional involvement, in the final analysis Tchaikovsky protests too much and in so doing fails to achieve that complete identification with his material that is the crowning glory of *Eugene Onegin*.

What of Taneyev's subsequent criticism that he could not hear the symphony without involuntarily seeing the ballerinas 'Mme Sobesh-chanskaya or Gillert No. 2', which spoilt his pleasure in the many beauties of the work?[7] It is true that the lovely B♭ minor oboe theme from the slow movement might have come straight out of *Swan Lake* and that the dream-like portions of the first movement, the scherzo and trio, and even parts of the festive finale could have been used for the ballet. In his reply[8] Tchaikovsky asked why Taneyev should object to ballet music, and he was at a loss to understand why dance tunes should not be employed episodically in a symphony. Nor did he see why it must necessarily be a mistake for a symphony to have a programme – another implied criticism of Taneyev's. He stated that in his work he made use of the central idea of Beethoven's Fifth Symphony, which like so many Romantics he was convinced had a programme.

The point about the programme is not important one way or the other, but, although Tchaikovsky warmly refuted the criticism itself, Taneyev's remark about ballet music was unfortunate in two ways. First, it has been used ever since, by those more prone to quote received ideas than to think for themselves, to imply that Tchaikovsky's main claim to fame is his ballet music, a remark as silly as it would be if quoted in connection with Stravinsky, whose first great seminal works (unlike Tchaikovsky's) were in fact ballets. Secondly, Tchaikovsky himself took the remark to heart perhaps more than he would have admitted. For, with the exception of the revision of his Second Symphony, he settled down to writing, instead of symphonies, suites in which he could not be accused of defects in symphonic structure. As he always reacted excessively to criticism, it is possibly allowable to deduce that Taneyev's criticism was one – but only one – of the causes of the hold-up of the natural development of his symphonic technique for a number of years, though eventually his talent erupted again in volcanic fashion. On the other hand it could be argued that

[7] RF(1), p. 32.
[8] *ibid.*, pp. 33–5.

the fact that it was dormant so long immeasurably enhanced the quality of the symphonic lava when it finally did erupt.

It is significant, too, that it was at this period of profound self-dissatisfaction, after the composition of the Fourth but before the revision of the Second Symphony, that he wrote a letter about his own inadequacy at manipulating form which is so often and so muddle-headedly quoted out of context and used as a stick with which to beat the whole of his symphonic output:

> If I can't complain of the poverty of my imagination or powers of invention, nevertheless I've always suffered from my inability to cope with form. Only as a result of persistent labour have I now managed to bring it about that the form in my compositions more or less matches the content. In the past I was too slipshod ... the seams were always visible. That was a fundamental defect, and it was only over a period of years that I began little by little to improve, but my compositions will never be *formally immaculate* since I can only correct, but not entirely change, the basic essentials of my musical nature... All the same it gives me joy to see that I'm gradually progressing along the road to perfection [of my musical talent].[9]

It was soon after this that he rigorously cut, pruned and otherwise revised the Second Symphony. It is particularly odd that Taneyev, of all people, should have written to Modest some years after the composer's death that he much preferred the original version.

In the letter in which he had criticized the Fourth Symphony, Taneyev wrote as follows about *Eugene Onegin*, after comparing it favourably with the symphony:

> *Onegin* has given me so much enjoyment, I've spent so many moments of pleasure examining the score that it would be quite impossible for me to find a single defect in this music. A wonderful opera! And yet you say that you want to stop writing [music]. On the contrary it's more necessary for you to write now than it ever was. You've never written so well. Put to profitable use the fact that you have achieved such perfection.[10]

The delicacy with which Tchaikovsky depicts Tatyana's character and emotions is nowhere more apparent than in the letter scene, of which the kernel is the following phrase:

[9] RK, Vol. I, p. 378.
[10] See note 7 above.

Ex. 11

This is the quintessential Tchaikovsky. The downward scale, associated as it was in his mind with the 'Fate' motive from *Carmen* and later in the opera where it is used significantly – in a quite different form – in Lensky's aria just before his death in a duel with Onegin, is here as much associated with love as with the fact that this love is tragically fated never to be consummated. There may have been an additional subconscious influence here – that of 'Tu l'as dit', the great love-duet from *Les Huguenots* in G♭ major, which starts with a downward scale of a type which had also by this time impregnated Tchaikovsky's style. The typical flattened sixth in the second bar is another stylistic feature inherited from Meyerbeer, and it is perhaps worth recalling that it was only a month or two before composing the letter scene that Tchaikovsky had arranged for Mme von Meck that curious *Marche Funèbre* from Natalya's Meyerbeerian G♭ major *arioso* from *The Oprichnik*, where a similar flattened sixth is also to be found in the harmony.

Even more important is what Gerald Abraham has called 'a sort of motto-theme for the whole opera': the horn phrase starting at the third bar of Ex. 11. It is used to denote virginal (sometimes childhood) innocence or pure, honourable love and acts as a probably subconscious but none the less successful unifying feature of the opera.[11] Although Tchaikovsky has made this little motto-theme so much his own, divorced from its context it is a commonplace enough phrase. A possible influence from the opening of Meyerbeer's 'Tu l'as dit' has already been mentioned. Further on in the same duet occurs the following passage:

---

[11] This can be verified by consulting EO(2), pp. 146–7 and referring Dr Abraham's useful quotations to their place in the score.

Ex. 12

The similarity between this and bars 3 and 4 of Ex. 11 will not escape notice, even down to the prominent use of the horn.

The descending scale is used much more chromatically elsewhere in the letter scene and, taken from that passage, in the monothematic introduction (Ex. 13(a)). This is very close indeed to the song 'Why did I dream of you', composed soon after Tchaikovsky first obtained the score of *Carmen*, from which the 'Fate' motive (Ex. 13(b)) is also quoted for purposes of comparison (see p. 80).

The *Carmen* motive has, naturally enough, been freely adapted and transformed, but the obvious similarities cannot be considered fortuitous if one takes into account Tchaikovsky's passionate fondness for Bizet's opera. These derivations are not cited in order to prove that *Eugene Onegin* is a derivative opera. It is to Tchaikovsky's credit that, although *Onegin* is built upon the 'rock' of the experience of other composers, it is a completely original and highly subjective work quite unlike any opera of Bizet, Meyerbeer or anybody else.

Ex. 13

The finest music in the opera is associated with Tatyana, though the characters of some of the minor figures, such as Lensky, are carefully enough drawn. But the slanting of the whole opera towards Tatyana tends to detract from the importance of Onegin himself, and his music as a consequence was perhaps not as deeply felt by Tchaikovsky as it ought to have been if he was to adhere strictly to the original implications of Pushkin's poem. After all, the boorish bachelor, the self-loving philanderer of the beginning of the 'novel in verse', has been transformed by the end, when he sees the country girl who had loved him metamorphosed into a sophisticated princess, into a man capable of loving another. While not matching this conception, Tchaikovsky none the less does portray something of the irony of the situation by giving him, when he sings, 'Yes, yes, all doubt is gone! I love her as if I were a boy in spellbound passion', the selfsame melody as that in which Tatyana sang of her love for him at the beginning of the letter scene. This is a very happy instance of 'theme quotation' typical in French and Italian operas of the period.

The trimmings of the opera are also successful; for example, the charming folk choruses at the beginning and the ballroom dances without which no Russian opera of the period was deemed to be complete – even Mussorgsky had to insert a mazurka and polonaise when he revised *Boris Godunov*. Furthermore, the rather bucolic waltz composed for the scene of the ball given by the Larins at their house in the depths of the country in Act II contrasts with the delicate waltz *con dolcezza ed eleganza* during which, in the last act, Onegin first sees the transformed Tatyana in her new sophisticated surroundings and learns to his horror that she is now married. These and many other brilliant touches serve to make *Onegin*, considered as a whole work of art, one of the greatest of all operatic masterpieces and a high-water mark in Tchaikovsky's career, reached by a slow and somewhat erratically tidal process of development.

It was impossible to remain at this level for long before the tide, as it were, had inevitably to go out again; but before this happened the songs of Op. 38 were written. Two of these, 'Don Juan's Serenade' and 'Mid the din of the ball', are masterpieces written in the wake of the inspiration which produced *Onegin*. But much more important than these was another major work composed in the space of a month when Tchaikovsky was in a 'favourable mood' in which 'composition is sheer delight'.[12] He had been joined by Modest and had returned to Clarens from Italy in very high spirits; life was 'rose coloured', especially on the arrival of the handsome young Kotek (who was now studying the violin with Joachim). Before Kotek's arrival he had started work on a piano sonata, but it was not going well. Among other pieces he played over with Kotek was Lalo's *Symphonic Espagnole* which gave him 'great pleasure', as he wrote to Mme von Meck.[13] The 'freshness, lightness, piquant rhythms, beautifully and admirably harmonized melodies' inspired him to write a violin concerto, in which the Lalo-type Spanish element is not entirely lacking. It progressed with rapidity. The first movement 'enraptured'[14] Kotek and Modest and the finale created a 'furore' among them. The *Andante* was rejected and a new one written:[15] without Kotek 'I'd have been able to accomplish nothing'. The orchestration was finished by 30 March/11 April. Nothing could interfere with the elation produced by the composition of this work. Even Taneyev's damning remarks about the Fourth Symphony did not break the spell, and in any case he had sugared the pill not only by his laudatory remarks about *Eugene Onegin* but by his reports of the favourable reception of

[12] Letter to Mme von Meck of 10/22 March 1878, RK, Vol. I, pp. 246–7.
[13] *ibid*., pp. 249–50. See also Gerald Abraham's foreword to the Eulenburg miniature score, p. i *et seq*. (Gerald Abraham's translation)
[14] RL, p. 158.
[15] *ibid*., p. 159.

Francesca da Rimini at its first Petersburg performance on 11/23 March. Tchaikovsky, who had received a great deal of technical assistance from Kotek, would have liked to dedicate the concerto to him, but this was impossible, he later told Jurgenson, as it would have led to 'gossip'.[16]

The Violin Concerto is certainly proof of the composer's return to the joys of living from the depths of mental despair; but it was still composed in the aftermath of that despair, and was a positive reaction from it. It bubbles over with that *joie de vivre* which Tchaikovsky was experiencing at the time, from the opening orchestral melody which summons the listener's attention and, like the much more flamboyant melody which opens the B♭ minor Piano Concerto, never reappears. Tchaikovsky has gauged the capabilities of the violin with nice judgment. It is certainly stretched to its technical limits. But the charming lyricism of both the main themes in the first movement is matched by the orchestral accompaniment. The full orchestra is unleashed for any length of time only in the *ritornello* sections which punctuate the proceedings at judicious intervals. Altogether a formal balance is achieved of which even Mozart might have approved – and Tchaikovsky was writing to Mme von Meck at this very time of his god Mozart, that 'sunny genius' whose music 'moves me to tears'.

The *Andante canzonetta*, as we have seen, was written last. If the opening of the main melody is of the Russo-Italian type so typical of Tchaikovsky, the end of the first eight-bar sentence has a distinctly 'Spanish' flavour – including an augmented second – though in reality it is no more (or less) Spanish than Lalo's or Bizet's Spanish-type music. But whatever its prototypes, it is one of the most characteristic melodies Tchaikovsky ever composed, beautifully decorated on its reappearance and merging into the delightful anticipation of the first theme of the finale which only previous composition of that theme could have allowed. As John Warrack has written,[17] 'the side of the violin's character introduced with

Ex. 14

[16] R J, Vol. I, p. 43.
[17] EX, p. 52.

(which consists of hardly more than the little figure quoted, together with a couple of bars of semiquaver figuration linking it to its next statement) has a distinct folk element.' Mr Warrack might have added that this kind of thing is derived from Glinka's *Kamarinskaya*, the second theme of which is the following Russian folk-song:

A year or two later Tchaikovsky wrote of Glinka's 'astounding originality' in his *Kamarinskaya*, from which all succeeding Russian composers, including himself, continued to borrow the moment they had to develop a Russian dance tune.[18] This was done 'unconsciously'. Glinka was able to concentrate in 'one short composition what a dozen second-rate talents would have created only by the complete expenditure of their powers'. The second subject of the finale, also folk-like, is more of the Russo-gypsy variety. Gypsy violinists and gypsy string bands were very much in vogue in Russia at the time, and Tchaikovsky heard them often in restaurants if not elsewhere. This sparkling finale is no less effective than the finale of the Second Symphony, with which it is in some respects comparable.

The original dedicatee of the concerto, Leopold Auer, refused to play it because it was 'unviolinistic' – in other words too difficult – and it was not until 1881 that another violinist, the young virtuoso Adolf Brodsky, made his Viennese début with it in December of that year. Hanslick and the majority of the other critics wrote rather more than middlingly adverse reviews (Hanslick's reference to 'stinking music'[19] is well known), but the concerto had at least been started on its course as one of the 'classic' violin concertos of all time. It is perhaps significant that both Tchaikovsky's concerto masterpieces – the other is the first Piano Concerto – should have received their premières outside Russia.

By the time the orchestration of the concerto was finished at the end of March, Kotek had already left Clarens, and arrangements were being made for Tchaikovsky to return at last to Russia. Sasha, at first cool towards Tchaikovsky because of his 'desertion' of his wife, had

[18] Letter to Mme von Meck of 5/17 July 1880, RI, Vol. IX, p. 176.
[19] RN, p. 262.

now experienced her at first hand and was only too pleased that Anatol had removed her to Moscow. Tchaikovsky could now return to Kamenka and pick up the threads of his home life with his sister's family.

8

Emotional relaxation and creative torpor (1878–85)

When Tchaikovsky arrived at Kamenka on 11/23 April he found to his great pleasure that Sasha had prepared a separate cottage for him and his servant to live in where it would be 'pleasant' to work.[1] He was to have his meals in the 'big' house. This was to be all he could call 'home' for the next seven years or so and he was grateful to Sasha for her kindness. Anatol and Jurgenson were trying to put the divorce wheels in motion and Antonina wrote that she was willing to divorce him.[2] But in the autumn, when Tchaikovsky returned to Moscow and Jurgenson tried to hold her to her promise, she refused, alleging that Tchaikovsky's family were plotting against her. She was persuaded to leave Moscow – at a price. The following spring, when he was staying with his brother in St Petersburg, he returned one day to the flat to find her waiting for him. The distress this caused was considerably magnified when she rented the flat above and pestered him for money. During the course of the summer she wrote to him in the Ukraine demanding more money and utterly refusing a divorce. The following summer, however, she wrote consenting to a divorce but refusing to allow it to be on the grounds of adultery, thus making it impossible. He wrote to Mme von Meck that only to see her writing on the envelope made him sick. She accused his family of slanderous attacks upon her. The game she was playing was finally exposed by Jurgenson in the spring of 1881 when he wrote to Tchaikovsky: 'She is living with her sister at No. 20 and in No. 21 is their "brother" Bolkov.'[3] It transpired that, as a result of the ministrations of this gentleman, Tchaikovsky's wife had had a child whom she had placed in a foundling's home. (She subsequently had a string of illegitimate children.) At last there was to be comparative peace for Tchaikovsky though he later instructed Jurgenson to give her money if she was in

[1] RK, Vol. I, p. 297.
[2] RN, p. 182.
[3] RJ, Vol. I, p. 184

need, and to the end of his life she was to write him occasional letters which caused him distress.

On his return to Moscow in September 1878 Tchaikovsky fully intended to resign from his post at the Conservatoire. But he was unable to do this immediately, since Rubinstein was in Paris, fulfilling the function at the Exhibition that Tchaikovsky had declined. When Tchaikovsky was able to tender his resignation to him the following month, he paradoxically did not consider that Rubinstein protested enough, prepared as he had been to answer the expected remonstrations of the older man, who contented himself with commenting that the withdrawal of his name would cause the Conservatoire to lose 'prestige'.[4] An offer of a much easier but at the same time more lucrative post at the St Petersburg Conservatoire was rejected. When Tchaikovsky was offered the directorship of the Moscow Conservatoire after Rubinstein's death in Paris in 1881, he turned this down also, being unwilling to give up his freedom and possibly precipitate a crisis in his relationship with Mme von Meck, which was still vital to him emotionally as well as financially. Furthermore he well knew that she liked to think of him as 'to some extent *my* composer', as she wrote on more than one occasion, asking the strictly rhetorical question whether it was wrong to be thus 'jealous' of him. And in spite of 'financial losses', first referred to in 1881, resulting in the sale of her large estate of Brailov in the Southern Ukraine and the purchase of the much smaller Pleshcheyevo, she continued Tchaikovsky's annuity without demur.

With his resignation from the Conservatoire in October 1878 began Tchaikovsky's 'nomadic' existence, as he called it; he flitted about between Russia and western Europe, never staying for very long in any one place. He was still shy of making personal contacts. For example, he did not call upon Jurgenson or Saint-Saëns when he was in Paris early in 1879, and fled before meeting Colonne after that conductor had put on a performance of *The Tempest* which received a lukewarm reception. In a subsequent letter to Colonne he made not only lame but unnecessarily deceitful excuses. It was only later that he was to take part in the social life of artistic Paris. The next year, at Mme von Meck's expense, the Fourth Symphony was performed by Colonne in Paris. The middle two movements were successful and were repeated a month later, but the Paris audience was nonplussed by the first movement and the finale. Tchaikovsky's *amour-propre* was

[4]RK, Vol. I, p. 445.

1 The composer's birthplace at Votkinsky

2 Tchaikovsky's family
Seated Tchaikovsky's
mother, his sister
Alexandra (Sasha),
his brother Hippolyte,
his father. *Standing* Peter,
his sister Zinaïda,
his brother Nicholas

3 A letter from Tchaikovsky,
aged ten, to his parents

4 Balakirev in about 1870

5 Tchaikovsky in 1874

6 Nadezhda von Meck

7 Mme von Meck's house
at Brailov, from the lake

Paris 7 Mars 1888

Verehrter Herr Berger!
Ich komme in London
am 19ten an und werde
im Hotel Dieudonné, wie
Sie mir es gerathen haben
absteigen.
Die Violinsolo partie (sie
ist im 1sten Geigen partie
gedruckt) schicke ich Ihnen
heute. Auf baldiges
Wiedersehen.
Ihr ergebener
P. Tschaïkovsky

8 A letter from Tchaikovsky to Francesco Berger,
Secretary of the Philharmonic Society, London

9 Tchaikovsky in 1893

10 Portrait of Tchaikovsky by N. Kuznetsov, 1893

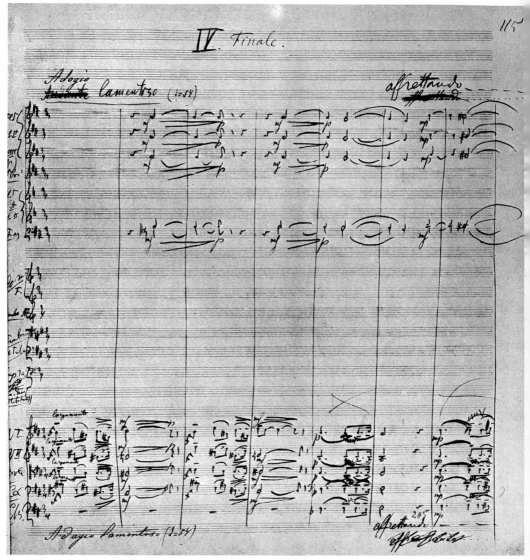

11 Autograph page of the opening of the Finale of the Sixth Symphony

wounded and he would not allow his benefactress to pay for the performance by Colonne of another work – the First Orchestral Suite – since he felt that paying for performances of his music in this way was sordid.

One acquaintance Tchaikovsky did make in 1880 was the Grand Duke Constantine Constantinovich, who greatly admired his music. Early in March the following year he met the Grand Duke and his cousins in Rome and was invited to visit Athens and Jerusalem with them. Unfortunately his imperial patrons had to end their holiday abruptly owing to the assassination of Alexander II, and Tchaikovsky himself had to go to Paris because of Rubinstein's sudden death there. Imperial patronage was to prove very useful to Tchaikovsky in the future. He was soon to be honoured with the Order of St Vladimir, and Alexander III was responsible for various commissions and was present at a number of dress rehearsals before first nights of Tchaikovsky's operas. The Tsar also attended the Petersburg première of *Mazeppa*,[5] expressing great surprise when Tchaikovsky himself was absent – though he had been present at the Moscow première a few days earlier. Tchaikovsky at this stage still hated crowds and had not yet emerged from the emotionally protective shell into which he had withdrawn in 1877. His main emotional outlet, especially in the late seventies and the early eighties, remained his effusive correspondence with Mme von Meck. At the end of 1878 she engaged rooms for him in Florence not too distant from her own villa, and they even caught a glimpse of one another – but no more. She never forced a meeting, much to his gratification, and they both revelled in this extraordinary Florentine 'honeymoon', so much more to Tchaikovsky's taste than the one he had had to endure the previous year. Mme von Meck administered to him only epistolary caresses. None the less he did occasionally crave for more, as when he told the newly married Anatol in 1882 of his unfulfilled need to be 'caressed' by a woman.[6] What he really required were the caresses not of a lover but of a mother. Pen contact with Mme von Meck was the nearest he was to get to this, and if he occasionally yearned for more, for the most part it proved sufficient – sufficient at any rate to obviate the necessity for other less Platonic caresses.

As early as the summer of 1878 Mme von Meck had lent him her

[5]RH, Vol. II, p. 622 *et seq.*
[6]RL, p. 279.

house at Brailov.[7] For a wonderfully happy fortnight the cares which still beset him at the time fell from his shoulders and he wallowed in the pleasurable sensations that the lush countryside evoked in him. He was periodically to be invited to stay by himself at Brailov and also at nearby Simaki, where he was given a small house he could occupy when Mme von Meck was herself resident at Brailov. Unfortunately on one such occasion in 1879 they met by mistake in the woods, greatly embarrassing each other. Tchaikovsky did not greet her verbally, confining himself to raising his hat, but she was not able to hide her confusion.

A musician who joined the von Meck household in the summer of 1880 and the two following summers was to become much better known than any other she had ever employed: the eighteen-year-old Claude Debussy, whose teacher Massenet was his 'hero', she told Tchaikovsky. She and Debussy played over piano-duet arrangements of the Fourth Symphony and the First Orchestral Suite and Debussy was 'delighted with the Fugue' in the suite.[8] In the autumn of 1880 Debussy took home with him, among other things, the score of *Romeo and Juliet*. It is perhaps even more revealing to learn that he arranged for keyboard the Spanish, Neapolitan and Russian dances from Act III of *Swan Lake*. Apparently Jurgenson published these arrangements which, Mme von Meck told Tchaikovsky, were not to bear the name of 'M. de Bussy' in case this would incur Massenet's displeasure.

Although Mme von Meck herself could never have a close personal relationship with Tchaikovsky, she had wished for some time to experience such a relationship at second hand, as it were, and to marry one of her children into the Tchaikovsky family. On 11/23 January 1884 her second son Nicholas and Sasha's daughter Anna Davydova were married in St Petersburg. (It had originally been intended by Mme von Meck that Nicholas should marry Anna's sister Vera, but in 1881 she married instead Alexei Rimsky-Korsakov.) Tchaikovsky's diaries become more detailed from the mid eighties onwards and the letters to Mme von Meck correspondingly less voluminous. But both contain periodic references to his health, to stomach pains, bilious attacks, sleeplessness, feverish headaches and the like. He had inadvertently written to her in the autumn of 1878 of 'fortifying' himself with wine, which she found 'dangerous', begging him not to remedy

[7] RN, pp. 185–6.
[8] See Edward Lockspeiser, *Debussy: His Life and Mind*, Vol. I (London, 1966), p. 46. Lockspeiser has a whole chapter on Debussy and the von Mecks, pp. 40–55, and Appendix A of this volume (p. 203) is a family tree of the von Mecks.

his ills in this way.[9] Henceforward references to secret tippling of brandy are in letters to the twins or in his diary. But he never became an alcoholic. His solitary potations were not compulsive, only a result of loneliness and boredom.

During the seven years between March 1878, when the Violin Concerto was completed, and April 1885, when the *Manfred* Symphony was started, Tchaikovsky struck a rich creative vein only once – in the year 1880. At the end of 1879, when he had already roughed out the Second Piano Concerto, but before he had written a fair copy of the two-piano version or orchestrated it, he first of all revised his Second Symphony and then started work on an Italian Capriccio. On 16/28 January 1880 he wrote to Mme von Meck from Rome: 'I want to write something in the manner of Glinka's Spanish Fantasias'[10] (*Jota Aragonesa* or Spanish Overture No. 1 and *Night in Madrid* or Spanish Overture No. 2). He was not affected at all by his father's recent death in St Petersburg, not even returning to Russia for the funeral. In fact the Italian Capriccio is one of his most joyful works. A week later he had finished the sketch: 'I think I can predict a good future for it. It will be effective thanks to the delightful [Italian] themes, which I managed to get hold of, partly from collections and partly from what I'd heard myself on the streets.'[11] The opening fanfare had its origins in a bugle call he heard each evening at a nearby cavalry barracks. He completed the instrumentation in May at Kamenka and Nicholas Rubinstein conducted the enormously successful first performance in Moscow at the end of the year. The critics praised it; but unfortunately critics since then have not always been so favourably disposed. Even more surprising are the accusations of 'Westernization' and even 'cosmopolitanism' which have been levelled at Tchaikovsky in this connection. He may have used Italian melodies, but his methods of development, or rather of repetitious interweaving, are very much in the Russian tradition – the tradition of the Glinka Spanish pieces, as he so rightly noted. The form of the Italian Capriccio is very similar to that employed by Glinka in *Night in Madrid*, which more than a decade earlier Balakirev had told Tchaikovsky to study for 'masterly fusing together of sections'.[12] In addition, Rimsky-Korsakov was to be influenced both by Glinka and by Tchaikovsky in his Spanish Capriccio of 1887 – one of three brilliant orchestral pieces which also included

[9]RK, Vol. I, p. 455.
[10]RN, p. 225.
[11]*ibid.*, pp. 225–6.
[12]See p. 27.

Sheherazade. Indeed he certainly learned something from Tchaikovsky's scintillating orchestral techniques in the Italian Capriccio; and there is very little to choose between the Spanish themes used by Glinka and Rimsky-Korsakov and the Italian themes used by Tchaikovsky. The truth is that all three works are in the same tradition, and none of them is in the least 'cosmopolitan'. If the Russians could adapt to their musical traditions the folk-songs of their own far-flung and extremely variegated empire, they could also adapt in a precisely similar manner Spanish or Italian folk-songs, or the folk-songs of other countries. For instance, Balakirev used Czech themes in his Czech Overture, and at one time even considered a symphonic poem on Greek themes.

Another golden work produced by Tchaikovsky 'from inner compulsion', as he wrote to Anatol, had started out as a symphony or string quintet,[13] but was turned in the end into a Serenade for String Orchestra, and according to the composer, the 'larger the string orchestra employed, the better'. From the outset this Serenade was a popular success. It received its first public performance under Nápravník, and was chosen by Anton Rubinstein for one of the concerts given in connection with the Moscow Art and Industrial Exhibition in the summer of 1882. Jurgenson wrote to Tchaikovsky in Kamenka on 31 May/12 June, the day after the performance:

> At the first rehearsal Jupiter [Anton Rubinstein] said to me: 'It seems to me that this is Tchaikovsky's best thing.' He has praised the piece to others equally unstintingly and at the 'dress' rehearsal he remarked: 'You can congratulate yourself on the publication of this opus.' The general public and musicians alike have taken it to their hearts.[14]

At last Anton Rubinstein had found a composition by his former pupil of which he wholeheartedly approved. Yet one cannot agree with Max Unger that the Serenade

> shows evidence of the influence of German classicism and romanticism upon Tchaikovsky to a greater extent than the majority of his other compositions. On hearing the first movement, with its heavily measured introduction, its first subject *à la* Schumann, and its old-fashioned second subject, a listener, unacquainted with the composer, would class him as a German Romantic reverting to archaic forms rather than a Russian master.

[13] RN, pp. 240–1.
[14] RJ, Vol. I, p. 249.

Particularly so with the second movement, a Waltz, which is characteristic of Johann Strauss with additional French grace.[15]

The influence of Schumann, as we have seen, is very important in Tchaikovsky's music and is hardly confined to the Serenade, while a much more 'old-fashioned' type of theme than that employed as the second subject occurs quite frequently throughout his work. After all, the difference between the adaptation of 'archaic' forms or themes on the one hand, and 'archaic' folk-songs on the other, to contemporary instrumental or operatic use is very small. In every case Tchaikovsky adapts them so thoroughly that they are entirely absorbed into his own style – a style as unmistakable in the Serenade as in the later symphonies, quite different though these were to be. In fact the *Allegro con spirito* main section of the finale of the Serenade bears a close resemblance to the finale of the Second Symphony. Both are based on short, repetitive folk-songs, both have an original second subject to act as a foil, both are developed in the manner of Glinka's *Kamarinskaya*. Moreover, the Russian folk-song in the finale of the Serenade provides the basis for the whole work, derived as it is from a simple descending scale. The fact that the strong, broad *marcatissimo* descending theme of the introduction to the first movement has its roots in the folk-song finale is strikingly demonstrated when they are juxtaposed towards the end of the finale. We have already observed how Tchaikovsky believed that any composer worth his salt should be able to construct suitable material from an arpeggio. Here he shows that a simple scale can provide equally suitable material. Other subjects in the Serenade delicately adapted to a descending scalic passage are the 'old-fashioned' second subject of the first movement, and the second subject of the entirely un-Strauss-like Waltz. In contrast to these, the beginning of the first subject of the Waltz and the important opening bars of the third movement, Elegy, are based on ascending scale passages. 'It is only talent that counts ... and enables beautiful music to be created out of nothing.' Tchaikovsky has done just that here.

One of the most important aspects of the Serenade is the superb writing for strings. In writing for the medium, Tchaikovsky shows technical prowess and insight that not even that wizard of the full orchestra, Rimsky-Korsakov, could match when writing for strings alone, and of his Russian contemporaries only Borodin could equal him. Where a full sound is required,[16] the layout of the score, double-

---

[15] Foreword to the Eulenburg miniature score, November 1926.
[16] As in the Elegy, bar 43, Eulenburg miniature score, p. 32.

stopping and so on is impeccable, naturally. But even more remarkable is the restraint shown in writing in two or three real parts, with consequent delicate doubling, as in the return of the first theme of the Waltz.[17] How different this is from the return of the second subject in the slow movement of the Fifth Symphony,[18] with hysterical octave doublings in the strings accompanied by suitably loud splutterings in the accented brass, the *fff con anima* becoming *con desiderio e passione*, then *con tutta forza* and finally *ffff*. Such recapitulatory *fortissimo* octave doublings and their concomitant skirls and blasts from the woodwind and brass are typical of Tchaikovsky in one mood, but no more typical than the restrained doublings and spare conception employed so often in the Serenade and elsewhere by a very different Tchaikovsky, able to reveal a *finesse* of feeling as distinguishing as the throbbing exultation and uncontrollable despair which in other periods of his life were portrayed so vividly in his music. It is this *finesse* above all else that would have been particularly appreciated by that pillar of musical refinement and urbanity, Anton Rubinstein.

Although other compositions were partially successful, the Italian Capriccio and the Serenade for Strings were the only works composed during the period from 1878 to 1885 in which Tchaikovsky achieved excellence throughout. At the other end of the scale were the *pièces d'occasion*, composed to order and uniformly feeble in content if not in volume. Of the bombastic *1812* Overture, written at the same time as the Serenade for Strings, it will suffice to let Tchaikovsky himself speak: 'The Overture will be very loud and noisy, but I've written it without affection and enthusiasm, and therefore there will probably be no artistic merit in it.'[19] Among many other commissioned works were a March and a Cantata, *Moscow*, composed for the coronation of Alexander III in 1883, and a simplified version of the *Slavsya* from Glinka's *A Life for the Tsar*, linked with the contemporary Russian national anthem. Alexander made it known that he would be pleased if Tchaikovsky composed some church music. The result was the *Three Cherubic Hymns* (1884), the *Hymn to St Cyril and St Methodius* and Six Church Songs for four-part chorus (1885). Another church music chore which he carried out, this time for Jurgenson, was the editing and arranging of the church music of Bortnyansky (1881); he freely admitted that he 'loathed' Bortnyansky's music. But one religious

---

[17] E.M.S., p. 25.
[18] *Andante mosso*, bar 142, E.M.S., p. 99.
[19] RN, p. 242.

work he did compose with love was the *Liturgy of St John Chrysostom* (1878). Tchaikovsky disliked church dogma but he was attracted to the beauty of the Liturgy. His setting is very simple, with the melody for the most part accompanied by plain harmonies. This, he well knew, was necessary to suit the puritanical tastes of the Russian Orthodox hierarchy, who were nevertheless furious when it was given a public concert performance, since they maintained that the liturgy was for use in church only. Tchaikovsky was very hurt by their attitude, for he had composed the work with genuine fervour.

Much of the music not composed to the order of others was written for himself. He wrote to Mme von Meck on 24 June/7 July 1878: 'I consider it to be an artist's *duty* never to give up, for *laziness* is a very strong human trait. Nothing is worse for the artist than to submit to it. Nor should he wait for inspiration. She is not the sort of visitor to like calling upon the lazy; she presents herself to those who summon her.'[20] The inspiration he had summoned in vain to assist him with the composition of his Piano Sonata in G major took him over heart and soul instead for the composition of the Violin Concerto in March 1878. The Piano Sonata was not completed until the summer (26 July/7 August) and it must be confessed that before its resumption inspiration must have flown out of the window. Tchaikovsky had no illusions about it himself. Writing on 29 October/10 November 1879 he tells Mme von Meck that Nicholas Rubinstein performed superbly 'this rather dry and complicated piece'.[21] 'Inspired' by Rubinstein's performance of his sonata, and of the originally spurned First Piano Concerto, Tchaikovsky proceeded to work vigorously on a second Piano Concerto, already started with the sole intention of staving off the boredom which invariably overwhelmed him if he did not have enough work in hand.[22] But once again, with the concerto only roughed out, real inspiration came his way in the form of the Italian Capriccio, and the orchestration was not completed until 28 April/10 May 1880. The work was dedicated to Nicholas Rubinstein. The dedicatee was careful not to repeat his earlier error and ruffle the composer's feelings to too great an extent, but he did comment on the episodical nature of the piano part. Unfortunately his untimely death meant that the première of the concerto had to be postponed until Taneyev had learnt the part.

[20] RK, Vol. I, p. 372.
[21] RI, Vol. VIII, p. 403.
[22] *ibid.*, pp. 389–90.

Anton Rubinstein conducted the first performance in May 1882 at a different concert in the same series as that in which he conducted the Serenade for Strings. The favourable comments he accorded the Serenade were not forthcoming for the concerto, and for once his views were right. The inordinately long first movement, the dull and uncharacteristic *Andante* which is almost a triple concerto, so prominent are the solo violin and cello parts, and the finale with its Schumannesque ♪♪ ♫ second subject in the relative minor – none of this adds up to more than a great deal of padding with contrived themes and for the most part boring decoration. There is not one melody comparable in any way with the plethora of beautiful tunes in the First Concerto, and it is no good trying to pretend that the riches of that work are matched in the Second. It is interesting to speculate why this is so, and why all Tchaikovsky's small-scale piano works, not least those of this period – the twenty-four children's pieces, the Six Pieces, Op. 51, and the Impromptu-Capriccio – are equally second rate. The answer may lie in the fact that he was incapable of being inspired by the piano as an instrument. (Berlioz was similarly deficient.) The success of the First Piano Concerto can be attributed to the fact that he was not thinking in terms of the piano at all, but of the orchestra. All the themes are conceived in their orchestral form (Tchaikovsky told Mme von Meck that he always composed with instrumental colouring in mind), and the piano, even if it introduces a theme, is merely having an arrangement, however good, of an orchestral conception. For example, all the themes in the lovely slow movement are introduced by the orchestra – and with highly individual, often ravishing instrumentation; even the curious little French tune in the *Prestissimo* is allotted to the strings while the piano has lively accompanimental passages. It is clear that, after Rubinstein's severe strictures about the piano part in the First Concerto, Tchaikovsky in the Second was sincerely trying to compose in terms of the piano rather than the orchestra, and it may be that this was partially responsible for the manifest inferiority of the later work.

Tchaikovsky's next work for piano and orchestra, the Concert Fantasia in G major, Op. 56, (1884), provides additional material to support this view. The sprightly folk-like first subject of the opening *Quasi rondo* is conceived in terms of the woodwind, while the second subject, though announced by the piano, soon appears in much more typical guise in octaves on the strings. Exactly the same applies to the first subject of the second (and final) movement – a slow theme in the tonic minor of which the initial version for piano, though adequately arranged, is presented by the orchestra later in its original form. We know that this is likely to have been its original form, since Tchaikovsky at first intended it to be the first movement of his contemporary Third Orchestral Suite. This movement is entitled 'Contrasts' because the second subject, in contrast to the first, has the character of a quick Russian dance, of the type to be found in the court scene from Act III of *Vakula the Smith*. In 1884 Tchaikovsky was looking over this favourite opera with a view to revising it, and the contrasting slow first theme is of the Bellini-with-a-Russian-accent type to be found in *Vakula*. The 'dance' theme, in the major, is later ingeniously combined with the slow theme, whose mode has to be changed in order that the two may be fitted together. Although this change of mode tends rather to cheapen the slow theme, the eloquence and charm of the movement outweigh its defects. The same is true of the tripartite first movement. Here the sonata-form exposition and recapitulation are separated by a long section for piano based on entirely new material, and if this cadenza-like solo is somewhat rhetorical, it is hardly possible to explore the byways of late nineteenth-century music for piano and orchestra without coming across such matter. In spite of its defects, this two-movement 'suite' for orchestra with virtuoso piano *obbligato* does not deserve the almost total neglect into which it has fallen. In contrast with the Second Concerto its better moments do not have to be searched for beneath mountains of padding.

After the completion of *Eugene Onegin* in 1878 Tchaikovsky was convinced that this collection of 'lyrical scenes' would never be a stage success. Indeed it failed to make much of an impression on the public both at its first (student) performance at the Moscow Conservatoire in March 1879 and at its first professional performance at the Bolshoy Theatre in Moscow in January 1881. It did not begin its subsequent successful career until it appeared on the Imperial stage in St Petersburg in October 1884. Meanwhile Tchaikovsky had completed two operas composed with the object of achieving success with the general public.

The first of these was based on his own adaptation of Zhukovsky's translation of Schiller's *Jungfrau von Orleans*. While he could feel sympathy with Joan of Arc as the central character of the opera – just as he had sympathized with Tatyana in *Onegin* – he doubtless hoped to be able to compose an opera in the Meyerbeer tradition of the Paris Opéra with great crowd effects, coronation scene and so on. Not only Meyerbeer but his successor Gounod, whose scores he had recently been studying, was the progenitor of the opera, the later composer especially in the more sugary portions of the score of *The Maid of*

Orleans. It is highly significant that Tchaikovsky himself stated that he was deliberately attempting to free himself from Russianism in this opera. The result was colourless, with an almost total lack of that subjectivity which was vitally necessary if he was to compose convincing music. His self-identification with Joan makes itself felt only in the kernel of the whole opera, Joan's 'narrative' and the scene of her recognition in the second part of Act II, composed first – like the letter scene in *Onegin* – and before the libretto was completed. Other passages worth mentioning are the chorus of village maidens, redolent of Glinka at his most anaemic, which begins Act I, and Joan's aria of farewell to her village near the end of the act; the dances, and Agnes's Gounod-like *arioso* in Act II; and the king's first *arioso* in the finale of Act III, in which the true Tchaikovsky almost manages to force his way through. But the characterization of both the medieval French aristocrats and peasants is puppet-like. Contrary to Tchaikovsky's hopes the opera was an immediate failure, though the audience acclaimed the composer personally at the first performance on 13/25 February 1881. But it did achieve a result for which he was clearly anxious when composing it: it was his first opera ever to be performed outside Russia. It was produced on 16/28 July 1882, not in Paris but in Prague, in a Czech translation. Though the Czechs at that time, for political reasons, were pro-Russian to the point of hysteria, the opera was soon dropped from the repertory.

While still aiming for the box-office success which had so far eluded him, Tchaikovsky in his next opera did not attempt to expunge the Russian element which he well knew to be an essential characteristic. Indeed he had written to Mme von Meck as early as the spring of 1878 that he had been soaked in the wonderful beauty of Russian folk-song from his earliest childhood in the country: 'I am *Russian* in the completest possible sense of that word.' [23] There was ample opportunity for the introduction of Ukrainian and Russian folk-like themes, in the manipulation of which Tchaikovsky had shown such mastery in *Vakula*, in the opera *Mazeppa*, which he started writing at the beginning of June 1882 – for example, the folk-choruses and a *hopak* in Act I; but this music is here seldom satisfactorily integrated with the rest of the opera. The scene between the heroine Mariya and the hero-villain Mazeppa with which Tchaikovsky began writing the opera does not bear comparison with the letter scene from *Eugene Onegin*, equally central though it is to the plot. Nor does Tchaikovsky begin

[23] RK, Vol. I, p. 236.

to make the most of the tale, adapted from a libretto by V. P. Burenin based on Pushkin's *Poltava*. The opportunity for characterization afforded by the Ukrainian separatist Mazeppa is tremendous. Here is a man who at one and the same time is capable of singing tenderly of his (reciprocated) love for Mariya, and of torturing and executing the father of his loved one for the sake of his cause. He is actually singing of the beauty of the Ukrainian starlit night as his torturers are at their grisly labours in the dungeons below. Mussorgsky would have written perfect music for such scenes, and *Mazeppa* need not have taken second place even to *Boris Godunov*. But Tchaikovsky was not capable of identifying himself with such a character as Mazeppa, and dramatic truth is lacking in his opera, though he does achieve music of some distinction and even power. He might have been able to feel more passionately for Mariya, who discovers what her lover is about only at the scene of her father's execution, when she rushes on to the stage as the axe (and the curtain of Act II) falls, had she not been a rather secondary, negative character. She really comes to life only when she has gone out of her mind (after the battle of Poltava in which Peter the Great is victorious), as she sings a lullaby over the lover of her childhood days, Andrey, while he lies dying of a gunshot wound inflicted by the defeated Mazeppa. With this haunting D♭ major lullaby the opera ends. If such a dramatic masterstroke could have been matched elsewhere in the opera it might have risen above the commonplace.

Tchaikovsky wrote three orchestral suites between 1878 and 1884. The unique opportunity that gramophone records afford of hearing all three suites one after another leads one to the irresistible conclusion, long ago reached by public and conductors alike, if not by musicians generally, that the Theme and Variations that constitute the finale of the Third Suite is incomparably the finest movement in the suites as a whole. Indeed it sums up brilliantly what Tchaikovsky had been trying to achieve elsewhere in the suites, more often than not with only very moderate success. Not only the suites but all his best music between 1878 and 1885 was warm, cheerful and relaxed. There is no hint whatever of the emotional depths plumbed in the Fourth Symphony and again in the last years. There is no trace of the utter commitment with which the entire score of *Eugene Onegin* is impregnated. It is not that Tchaikovsky over and over again did not attempt to be thus committed, but merely that his subconscious recovery from the mental explosions of the mid seventies could not be hurried. Moreover some of the seemingly committed songs of Op. 47, dating from 1878, are but a pale reflection of what had been achieved in *Eugene Onegin*, even if 'If only I'd known', for instance, appears on the surface to involve the composer's feelings. The later group of songs, Op. 57, is almost uniformly poor. Not much better are the violin pieces entitled *Souvenir d'un lieu cher*, one of which is the discarded *Andante* from the Violin Concerto. Tchaikovsky told Mme von Meck that little pieces in general were 'sometimes tedious' to work on.[24]

Since 1880 he had been trying to get started on another symphony, and his diary of 1884 testifies to his growing wish to write one. On 16/28 April, while at Kamenka, he wrote: 'I've tried to lay the foundation of a new symphony... As I strolled in the garden it was not a future symphony but a suite which germinated in my mind.'[25] It is significant that during the ensuing composition of the predominantly joyous Third Suite there are many jottings in the diary about his thirteen-year-old nephew Vladimir, nicknamed 'Bob', such as: 'What a darling Bob is,', and 'My dear, incomparable, enchanting ideal Bob'.[26] Tchaikovsky's love for his nephew had not yet begun to involve him in appalling self-reproach, one of the results of which was to be the composition of that monumentally despairing work, the Sixth Symphony, dedicated to Bob.

If anything could have aroused Tchaikovsky emotionally in the early eighties it was surely the tragic death of Nicholas Rubinstein in Paris in 1881. In Rubinstein's memory he wrote a two-movement Piano Trio. This would have the additional advantage of pleasing Mme von Meck, for whose private piano trio he had been asked to write something some time before. It is impossible, however, to agree with Edwin Evans that the first movement, *Pezzo elegiaco*, 'compels one's sympathy' from the first note to the last or that 'the accents of deep sincerity are absolutely convincing'.[27] Sincerely sorry though he undoubtedly was about Rubinstein's death, it was of the effect upon himself that Tchaikovsky was really thinking. On arrival in Paris to attend the funeral he wrote to Modest: 'To my shame, I must own that I was suffering not so much from a sense of fearful, irretrievable loss as from the dread of seeing poor Rubinstein's body.'[28] As Colin Mason rightly pointed out, the first movement of the trio is in fact

---

[24] *ibid.*, p. 375.
[25] RN, p. 314.
[26] See EV, pp. 29, 30, etc.
[27] ES, pp. 156–7.
[28] RL, p. 268.

'rather heavy-handed'[29] with the undue prominence of the piano spoiling the balance. Tchaikovsky's elegy is only superficially convincing, and the same is true of the very long series of variations that comprise the second movement. A naïve theme associated with his friend is mercilessly put through its paces, each variation being said to be connected with some incident in Rubinstein's life. The emotional involvement of even the enormous final variation is more apparent than real, and despite some pages of well-wrought music, the overall effect of this inflated piece is of dullness – a defect for which Tchaikovsky of all people may not readily be excused.

[29]ER(5), p. 110.

9

Creative renewal 1885–8

The year 1885 was important for Tchaikovsky for two reasons. First, he decided to end his itinerant existence and rent a house of his own at Maidanovo, near Klin and within easy reach of Moscow. When at home he now adopted a routine from which he seldom deviated. He worked between half-past nine and one o'clock and between five and seven. But his most important creative work was done during his solitary afternoon walks when he jotted down ideas in notebooks. It was Balakirev who had originally advised a creative walk during the composition of *Romeo and Juliet*, and Tchaikovsky always found that this was a good way to stimulate ideas. With this home as his anchor he was to be able to conquer his fear of society to such an extent that he could sally forth into the world and conduct his own works not only in Russia but in western Europe and the United States of America as well. The second reason for the importance of the year 1885 was that at last, after a gap of seven years, he started work in earnest on his next symphony. And this work aroused him from the comparative creative torpor into which he had unwittingly sunk, notwithstanding the large number of works manufactured during those years.

It is perhaps not surprising that it was to the busy, bustling, interfering but dynamically magnetic Balakirev that this resurrection was due. For Balakirev, by giving Tchaikovsky real self-confidence in his supervision of the composition of *Romeo and Juliet* in the autumn of 1869, had been responsible for sparking off his first mature creative fire which continued to burn with ever-increasing intensity until the crisis-torn year 1877. The correspondence between the two men, which had lapsed owing to Balakirev's mental breakdown and subsequent withdrawal from public life in the early seventies, was resumed when Tchaikovsky wrote in 1881 about a new edition of *Romeo and Juliet*.[1] (In the original edition the dedication had been omitted.) Balakirev did not reply to Tchaikovsky's letter until a year later, by which time

[1] RA, p. 163.

he had received a score of *Romeo* with the dedication to him writ large upon the title-page. He expressed pleasure that Tchaikovsky had not forgotten him and said that he would like to give him 'the programme of a symphony which you would carry out splendidly ... Your apogee – this is your two symphonic poems – *The Tempest* and *Francesca da Rimini*, especially the latter'. He added characteristically: 'I trust I well understand where the strength of your talent really lies.'[2] In another letter Balakirev wrote down a programme Stassov had originally given him many years before on the subject of Byron's *Manfred*, inserting his own comments.[3] Tchaikovsky's reply was not enthusiastic, although he had at first expressed interest, and he absolutely disagreed that he had reached his 'apogee' in *The Tempest* and *Francesca*. But he wrote in very flattering terms to Balakirev all the same, totally contradicting a derogatory letter about the 'mighty handful' he had sent to Mme von Meck while he was still in the doldrums at the end of 1877.

It was not until Balakirev had seen him, during his visit to St Petersburg in October 1884 for the first performance on the Imperial stage of *Eugene Onegin*, that Tchaikovsky really seemed to warm to the idea, giving way to the urgent personal persuasions of Balakirev and putting on one side his original objections which had included his extreme fondness for Schumann's *Manfred* and his consequent inability to evoke other music than Schumann had provided for it. Balakirev sent him a revised programme, with elaborate details as to the keys that should be employed.[4] Tchaikovsky bought a copy of the poem and set off on the day after receiving Balakirev's letter for Davos in Switzerland, not primarily in order to obtain local Alpine colour for *Manfred*, but to visit Kotek who lay dying of tuberculosis. In spite of the aptness of the surroundings and the suitable Manfredian gloom induced by the extreme illness of 'Kotik', Tchaikovsky did not set to work at once on *Manfred*, though he read the poem and wrote promising Balakirev to do so. At Davos, in Paris whither he presently drifted, and in his new home at Maidanovo in February and March 1885, he revised *Vakula the Smith*, renaming it *Cherevichki*.

This opera has already been considered in some detail, but one further remark is worth making. In his revision Tchaikovsky added the Schoolmaster's song, and the recitative surrounding it, to the

[2] *ibid.*, p. 164.
[3] *ibid.*, pp. 165–7.
[4] EU, p. 118.

delightful slap-stick scene in Solokha's hut where, one after another, her lovers come to her and, on the arrival of the next one heralded by knocks on the door, each hides in a sack to escape detection. The Schoolmaster sings of his passion for her to an accompaniment (Ex. 15(a)) which is extremely like a passage in Balakirev's Musical Picture *1000 years* based on the folk-song 'It was not the wind' (Ex. 15(b)) – though it is more in the harmonic context of a passage already quoted from Balakirev's Czech Overture[5] (see examples on page 103).

The Schoolmaster's little mock folk-song which follows is similar to the folk-song which is the second subject of the *Allegro moderato* in *1000 years* with its sprightly rhythm in the first bar, including ♪♫, and its stamping rhythm in the second; and after the dramatic knocks on the door the Balakirevan harmonies employed by Tchaikovsky in ·the orchestral accompaniment to the recitative of the Schoolmaster, terrified that he will be discovered with the rather easy Solokha, all point to one inescapable fact: Tchaikovsky is writing a skit on the 'schoolmaster' Balakirev.

Having thus got rid of his feeling of pique towards Balakirev, in April he set to work with a will on the *Manfred* Symphony rather than on a projected opera based on Shpazhinsky's drama *The Sorceress*, aided in his resolution by the fact that the libretto which was being prepared by Shpazhinsky had not yet arrived. Just as the genesis of the Fourth Symphony had caused him some difficulty, so the labour involved in what turned out to be a programme-symphony of enormous proportions induced a depressed and overwrought state of mind. Not since 1877 had he known this kind of creative pressure. On 13/25 September he wrote to the delighted Balakirev that his wish had been fulfilled and *Manfred* was finished: 'Of course I'm unable to foresee whether or not I'll please you in this symphony, but *believe me* that never in my life have I laboured to such an extent and so fatigued myself with work.'[6] After it had been completed and engraved he told Jurgenson that he valued it very highly: 'I'm possibly mistaken, but it seems to me that it is the best of my compositions.'[7]

He repeated this remark almost word for word to Mme von Meck after the first performance at an R.M.S. concert in Moscow on 11/23 March 1886.[8] By September 1888 he had completely changed his mind

[5] See Ex. 9(a) (p. 59).
[6] RA, p. 176.
[7] RJ, Vol. II, p. 31.
[8] RK, Vol. III, p. 410.

Ex. 15

and told the Grand Duke Constantine that it was 'abominable'.[9] But by this time he had already written his Fifth Symphony which, being newly composed, far outshone its predecessor in his view. However, by December 1888, owing to its unfavourable reception by the critics, he was reviling his Fifth Symphony just as much as he had reviled the *Manfred* Symphony a few months before, announcing to Mme von Meck that there was in it something repellent, a certain gaudiness, insincerity and artificiality. And he appended a note that would undoubtedly please his 'best friend': 'Yesterday evening I looked over

[9]RN, p. 453.

the Fourth Symphony, *ours*! What a difference, how superior, how much better it is!'[10] Perhaps to change his mind is a composer's as well as a woman's privilege. Tchaikovsky's epistolary eulogies or condemnations of his own works are not to be taken too seriously, nor should they be quoted out of context. His desire to please the particular recipient of the letter must always be taken into account. He once admitted in his diary that in his letters he tended to 'pose', and that the letters of the celebrated are frequently not 'entirely sincere'.[11]

Balakirev considered the *Manfred* Symphony to be Tchaikovsky's masterpiece. It was certainly his finest symphony up to that time and is in no way inferior to its better-known successor. The sincerity of this convincingly subjective composition is manifest, and its lack of showiness can be attributed to the good taste of the man to whom it was to be dedicated, together with a fear of Balakirev's sharp rebuke should it in anyway fall short. Hence the beautiful soft ending with held woodwind chords and *pizzicato* strings, unlike the 'sudden thumped' chords which Balakirev had deprecated in *Romeo and Juliet* but like the close of Balakirev's *1000 years* – and similar to the end of Schumann's *Manfred* Overture. Another Schumannesque-Balakirevan influence is to be found at the beginning of the pastoral third movement in the use of the sharpened dominant over a tonic pedal producing a transition to the relative minor (Ex. 16(a)). This was a favourite idiom of Balakirev's, who employed it in the middle section of his piano fantasy *Islamey*, for instance. For an example by Schumann one has to look no further than his *Manfred* Overture (Ex. 16(b)). Rimsky-Korsakov imitated Tchaikovsky's example at the beginning of the third movement of his *Sheherazade*.

All the formal aspects of writing such a programme-symphony are thoroughly understood, not the least of which is the successful inclusion of the motto-theme in very different orchestral contexts; this theme itself,[12] derived as we have seen from one of Tchaikovsky's most important melodic formulae based originally on folk-song, is presented in much more sombre surroundings than ever before. The pervading gloom of the first and last movements is imaginatively contrasted with the idyllic pastoral third movement and, perhaps the crowning achievement, a scherzo of unsurpassed delicacy combined with verve

[10] RK, Vol. III, p. 559.
[11] RG and EV, entry for 27 June/9 July 1888.
[12] See Ex. 5(b) on p. 38 for a quotation of its opening and a comparison with other similar themes.

Ex. 16

depicting, according to the programme, the Alpine fairy, appearing to Manfred in the rainbow from the spray of a waterfall. Rimsky-Korsakov, though he obviously studied the orchestration of this movement with great care, never achieved a charm quite so elusive, an effect quite so unobtrusively varicoloured.

With *Manfred* off his chest, Tchaikovsky started on *The Sorceress*. The first act was finished in three weeks, but the rest of the opera was not finally ready for Jurgenson's engraver until May 1887. Nothing much happens in the first act, and as a result Tchaikovsky was able to set the scene with appropriate music of a folk-like nature, the centre-piece of which is a superb aria sung by the main character, Natasya (nicknamed 'Kuma', the 'gossip'). In much of the rest of the opera a pseudo-realism is attempted in which Tchaikovsky, in the character of an operatic hack striving for success with the multitudes, fails as overwhelmingly as he had always failed before in such a role when his own personal feelings remained uncommitted. Owing to the objections which the prima-donna made, on reading the original play, to singing the role of a woman of too obviously unredeemably loose morals, certain of Kuma's roughnesses had to be somewhat smoothed out, resulting in a character less like Carmen than Tchaikovsky would have wished, and with whom he failed to identify himself. The opera was an immediate failure, no less wounding to his pride than it was thoroughly deserved.

It was at the end of 1886 that he plucked up enough courage to ascend the conductor's rostrum for the first time for nearly ten years, for the rehearsals of *Cherevichki*. He conducted the first performance on 19/31 January 1887 after suffering dreadful mental torture all day. His conducting was very favourably reviewed and he even managed to conduct a second performance soon after hearing of the sad death of Sasha's daughter Tatyana,[13] a drug addict who had had an illegitimate son in Paris in 1883 (later to be adopted by Nicholas). After this success he determined to conduct a concert of his own works in St Petersburg. Of the first rehearsal on 28 February/12 March he wrote in his diary: 'Nervousness, terror. Then nothing. Ovation from the artists.'[14] On 3/15 March he noted that his rehearsal was attended by 'Balakirev and his entourage'. On the next day he went to a musical evening at Balakirev's and on the 5th the concert was a triumph. But he offended Balakirev by leaving St Petersburg on the day before the latter's concert celebrating the twenty-fifth anniversary of the foundation of the Free School of Music. Balakirev did not answer Tchaikovsky's note of apology.[15]

In the autumn he conducted the first performance of *The Sorceress*. While the opera itself was a failure, his conducting was announced by Cui to be 'excellent, first-class',[16] and a first all-Tchaikovsky concert conducted by the composer in Moscow on 14/26 November was so enthusiastically received that it had to be repeated *in toto* the next

[13]RN, pp. 400–1.
[14]RG and EV, entry for 28 February. Also RN, p. 405.
[15]RA, p. 183.
[16]RN, p. 426.

day.[17] At this concert the first performance took place of a suite consisting of arrangements for orchestra of some of Mozart's lesser piano pieces and an adaptation of Liszt's arrangement of *Ave verum corpus*. This Fourth Suite (*Mozartiana*) had been arranged during a holiday with Anatol, who was now stationed in the lovely Georgian town of Tiflis in the Caucasus – where the local branch of the R.M.S. had fêted Tchaikovsky the previous year. Its rapturous reception led to other such concoctions by Russian composers, such as Balakirev's Suite on Pieces by Chopin.

A month after this success Tchaikovsky set out on the first of a series of conducting tours of the west. He visited Berlin, then Leipzig, where on New Year's Day 1888 at the house of his fellow countryman Brodsky occurred his famous meeting with Brahms, whose personality he found more agreeable than his music, the 'puzzling' English composer Ethel Smyth, and Grieg, with whom he was in complete sympathy.[18] Here he conducted his First Suite, from which it is particularly revealing to note that the critics singled out for praise the first-movement fugue. After Hamburg, where the well-meaning Avé-Lallement, aged chairman of the committee of the Philharmonic Society, lectured him on his noisy orchestration and barbarous musical education, he returned to Berlin to conduct a concert and then set out by way of Leipzig for Prague. In Prague he met Dvořák, to whom he instantly took a liking. His concerts were used as occasions for pro-Russian demonstrations, but it was difficult for him not to be pleased with the ovations, and he was particularly delighted at the 'tremendous success' of the 'splendidly staged' second act of *Swan Lake*.[19]

His music was also warmly received in Paris and London, where pro-Russian feelings were not exactly at their nadir, but his social acceptance in Paris – where he met, among others, Gounod, Fauré, Massenet and Widor (an 'excellent organist'[20]) was not matched in London, the foggy climate of which depressed him, and he was only too pleased to leave for his brother's Tiflis house and the glorious climate of the Caucasus. On the way back to Russia he went to a performance of Gilbert and Sullivan's *The Mikado* in Vienna. He could 'hardly endure two-thirds of one act'.[21]

---

[17] *ibid.*, p. 428.
[18] RG, p. 370 *et seq.*
[19] RN, p. 440.
[20] *ibid.*, p. 444.
[21] *ibid.*, p. 445.

10

The last years 1 (1888–90)

In a letter to Modest from Tiflis Tchaikovsky revealed that he was considering as an opera subject Pushkin's *Queen of Spades*. For the time being, however, the subject did not sufficiently 'move' him. But 'in the course of the summer I shall *definitely write a symphony*'.[1] After his holiday in Tiflis, instead of returning to Maidanovo, he settled in a new house at Frolovskoye between Klin and Moscow. This little house was set in the midst of beautiful woods and had a lovely garden the cultivation of which interfered with the composition of the symphony, so he said. Despite this, between 19/31 May and 22 June/4 July he had finished the short score not only of the Fifth Symphony but of a new programme work, the Overture-Fantasia *Hamlet*. The orchestration of both occupied him on and off until October, when *Hamlet* was completed.[2] He had successfully conducted *Romeo and Juliet* several times on his tour, and he was anxious to compose a companion work which he could dedicate to Grieg. But a further reason lay behind the simultaneous composition of *Hamlet* and the Fifth Symphony. He knew well enough that Balakirev would not approve of the symphony, but a work similar to *Romeo and Juliet* was another matter. When he arrived in St Petersburg to conduct the first performance there, he immediately sent off a score of *Hamlet* to Balakirev (letter of 8/20 November 1888) in the hope that 'it will please you'.[3] And that he had the *Manfred* Symphony in mind when he started composing *Hamlet* is borne out by the fact that on the first page of his autograph sketch the following is written: 'Do something at the beginning to avoid its being too similar to the beginning of Manfred'[4] – but it does resemble the beginning of *Manfred* all the same.[5]

In other respects it is naturally *Romeo and Juliet* and not *Manfred*

[1] RL, p. 400.
[2] RH, Vol. III, p. 319.
[3] RA, p. 184.
[4] RN, p. 449; photographs of manuscript, *ibid.*, p. 515.
[5] See Exs. 5(b) and 5(d) on p. 38.

that the new work resembled – to such an extent, as it turned out, that it tends to repeat in a rather stereotyped manner the shape, form and even basic content of the earlier work. Balakirev pencilled in the margin of the score against what is usually called the love-theme: 'Hamlet pays Ophelia compliments, and presents her with an ice-cream.'[6] Even if this cruel remark is unfair, it must be confessed that the theme bears no comparison with the love-theme in *Romeo and Juliet* which had pleased Balakirev so much nineteen years before, and that *Hamlet* is a mere feeble, though not tinselly, repetition of past mannerisms.

In one important formal aspect the Fifth Symphony could hardly have been as successful without the experience gained in the *Manfred* Symphony. We have noted how, in spite of Tchaikovsky's programme sent to Mme von Meck, his 'Fate' motive in the Fourth Symphony is not really the 'germ of the whole symphony'. That he had a very similar programme in view for the Fifth Symphony is borne out by the following incomplete jotting: 'Introduction. Complete resignation before Fate, or, which is the same, before the inscrutable predestination of Providence. Allegro (I) Murmurs, doubts, lamentations, reproaches against XXX. (II) Shall I throw myself into the embraces of Faith???'[7] Tchaikovsky had successfully obeyed Balakirev's instruction to introduce Manfred's motto-theme into all the movements of the *Manfred* Symphony. The 'Providence' motive heard at the beginning of the Fifth Symphony is not only satisfactorily introduced into the other movements but, much more important, pervades the whole work. Nothing that he had achieved in the Fourth Symphony could have provided a preliminary exercise for such an achievement. The construction of the motive is extremely skilled. It will be seen that it is based on a simple arpeggio of E minor at (a) of Ex. 17, with a typical alternating tonic-subdominant accompaniment, followed by a downward scale at (b), accompanied by an upward scale. We have seen how Tchaikovsky was capable of constructing themes from scales and arpeggios in the past, and here his skill is used in the writing of a cyclic symphony. For example, the important transition theme of the first movement is based on an upward scale passage, while the Valse and the second subject of the finale begin with downward scale passages, and the second subject of the slow movement derives from an arpeggio – and so on.

[6]RA, p. 203.
[7]From a note-book in the Tchaikovsky Museum at Klin. Quoted in EX, p. 29, and EY, p. 289.

Ex. 17

The Fifth Symphony is even more operatic in nature than the Fourth. Besides the highly coloured orchestration and the vivid presentation of the ideas, the operatic crescendos may be instanced, together with even more frequent alterations in tempo than ever before, especially in the slow movement, where the 'licence' of the operatic aria is established at the outset, *Andante cantabile, con alcuna licenza*, and the *licenza* is marked in the score: *animando, ritenuto, sostenuto, con moto, poco più animato* and so on, every few bars. Another important point of style which aids Tchaikovsky's predilection for contrasts is exemplified in his scoring for contrasting blocks of similar instruments, as in the first D major theme from the second group of the first movement.[8] The symphony abounds in dramatic contrasts. The sudden introduction, after a brief *stringendo crescendo*, of the 'Providence' motive into the heart of the slow movement provides only one of many fine examples.

It is the finale with which many knowledgeable commentators have found fault, starting with Brahms (who stayed behind an extra day in

[8] Eulenburg miniature score, p. 20 (bar 154).

Hamburg especially to hear Tchaikovsky conduct the symphony early in 1889). Donald Tovey, the king of the 'Brahminen', followed suit. It is worth while examining the reasons Tovey gives for its failure. He refers to 'the problems of getting up any sense of movement in a finale at all', and states that his *locus classicus* for impotence in that matter is the finale of Tchaikovsky's Fifth Symphony. If the composer had intended to produce the nightmare sensation, or the Alice-and-Red-Queen sensation, of running faster and faster while remaining rooted to the spot, he might have been said to have achieved his aim here.' While 'you must not expect Bruckner to make a finale "go" ... the popular Tchaikovsky is in worse case than Bruckner, for he evidently expects his finales to "go" ... Tchaikovsky's finale [of the Fifth Symphony] wants to go and cannot'.[9]

John Warrack adduces a different reason for the alleged failure of the finale. The symphony appears on the surface to have the 'strife-to-victory' programme, since the finale opens with the 'Providence' motive in the major key and closes with the first subject of the first movement, also in the major key, blasted forth in a trumpet fanfare, *ffff*. Enclosed within is a seemingly joyful movement, but Warrack rightly states that

> there remains something unconvincing in this triumph ... What has transpired, one asks, to alter the issue of resignation before Providence so completely? ... Until the finale, the symphony has embodied a nature fundamentally unhappy but brought into a state of equilibrium. Now for the first time a note of falseness, of overstatement, enters into the music; and although it is all bravely carried through, the final triumph cannot help seeming hollow.[10]

Of course Tovey and Warrack are right. But surely their arguments both point to a very different conclusion than the one they have reached. If the finale had 'got' anywhere and an escape had been made from 'Fate' or 'Providence', if the triumph had been achieved, then the symphony as a whole would have been much less successful. Tovey's very apt analogy of the 'nightmare sensation' of 'running faster and faster while remaining rooted to the spot' is just what leaves us with the feeling that we can never escape from our 'Fate'. Tchaikovsky is giving the impression of trying to go and failing. The hysterically overstated endeavour to produce 'triumph', which in the end only sounds 'hollow' and false, leaves the impression of the

[9] EW (1), p. 60.
[10] EX, pp. 32–3.

inescapably overwhelming power of 'Fate' and the uselessness of the fight against it, however hard that fight may be and however successful the apparent outcome. The effect of the Fifth Symphony is therefore one of failure to resist the inevitable power of Destiny in spite of monumental struggle and even temporary success.

One cannot pass over the Fifth Symphony without a brief comment on Tchaikovsky's continuing and developing use of the symphonic march and the symphonic waltz. The Valse which replaces the more usual scherzo as the third movement seems to be no more than a charming example of the type adumbrated by Berlioz in the *Symphonie Fantastique* and to be found in Tchaikovsky's own Second Suite, but its apparent innocuousness is belied by the derivation of its initial motive from the 'Providence' theme and by the introduction of that theme itself during its course, which gives to the proceedings a touch of the sinister. Much less delicately sinister is the threatening march which constitutes the first subject of the first movement and pervades much of the movement. Nor does its flamboyant emergence in the major at the end of the finale in any way detract from its inherently sinister quality. This is surely a prodigious feat, however subconscious this particular aspect of the idea may have been during the composition of the work. In the final analysis the Fifth Symphony is one of the finest cyclic works of the nineteenth century.

Meanwhile Tchaikovsky had completed a set of six songs to French texts, op. 65, dedicated to Désirée Artôt-Padilla, whom he had met again in Berlin the previous winter and found 'as fascinating as ever', as he wrote to Modest.[11] Fascinating though she may have continued to be, the songs are as feeble as the earlier works he had dedicated to her, and the six songs, Op. 63, dedicated the previous year to the Grand Duke Constantine, are equally devoid of character. And only one of the twelve songs, Op. 60, dating from 1886, is of a slightly less empty character, the 'Song of the Gypsy girl'. After the songs dedicated to Artôt this annual outburst of vocal vacuity ended for good. (Tchaikovsky's only other songs were a group of six composed in the last year of his life and were of a much higher standard.) Another occasional piece was composed the previous year (1887) in response to a request from a cellist friend, Anatol Brandukov. It was the *Pezzo Capriccioso* for cello and orchestra. Tchaikovsky did not allow its publication by Jurgenson until his old friend Fitzenhagen, dedicatee of

[11]RL, p. 391.

the Rococo Variations, had looked over the cello part.[12] The piece, in B minor, is of the *Sérénade Mélancholique* type and is not a *scherzando* caprice.

The Fifth Symphony was the first really important work to be composed after the *Manfred* Symphony. *The Sorceress*, the songs and the piece for cello and orchestra are all, comparatively speaking, quite insignificant. It is a tribute to the complete mental self-control Tchaikovsky had now achieved that he himself elected to conduct the first performances both of the symphony and of *Hamlet* in the more reserved atmosphere of the northern capital rather than in Moscow, his home ground. As far as the symphony was concerned, the orchestra and audience were enthusiastic, but the critics less so. Cui utterly failed to comprehend it. He was still full of Rimsky-Korsakov's recently performed Spanish Capriccio and had already looked over the scores of the Russian Easter Festival Overture and *Sheherazade*, both to be given for the first time the following month. In comparison with Rimsky-Korsakov's, Tchaikovsky's music as exemplified in the symphony was 'without character, routine stuff'.[13] By the time this acid review appeared, however (17/29 November), Tchaikovsky was already in Prague to conduct not only the symphony but *Eugene Onegin*, which was given there with enormous success on 24 November/6 December.

On his return to Moscow Tchaikovsky conducted the symphony there. And he had no sooner sketched out a great deal of a three-act ballet entitled *The Sleeping Beauty*, commissioned by Vsevolozhsky, the Director of the Imperial Theatres, and begun the previous October, than he set off on a second tour of the West, conducting in Cologne, Frankfurt, Dresden, Berlin, Leipzig, Geneva and Hamburg.[14] After another appearance in 'foggy' London, he started his leisurely return journey, embarking on the *Cambodge* at Marseilles, steaming through the Straits of Messina, and going ashore at the Greek island of Syra, at Smyrna and at Constantinople before reaching Batum en route for Anatol's place in Tiflis. On his tour, during the voyage and on his return home he continued work on the third act of *The Sleeping Beauty*. The short score was completed at Frolovskoye on 26 May/7 June, and the summer was spent in orchestrating it. He told Mme von Meck that he considered it one of his best compositions and that he was finding orchestration more difficult than formerly.[15] It cannot be

[12] R J, Vol. II, p. 68.
[13] R N, p. 458.
[14] R N, p. 463 *et seq.*
[15] R K, Vol. III, p. 580.

said that his instrumentation in previous works is not rather more than adequate – in many of them it is not only brilliant but astonishingly original. What is new is an even greater striving for exactness of orchestral effects – perhaps a result of his new experience as a conductor. It is significant that concerning Rimsky-Korsakov's Spanish Capriccio, which to some extent was indebted to him, he wrote to the composer: 'It is a colossal masterpiece of instrumentation.'[16] But it was not so much in the score of *The Sleeping Beauty*, beautiful though it is, as in the Symphonic Ballad *The Voyevoda*, conceived the following year, that this concern for instrumentation had so taken over in the creative process that, without the orchestral colouring, only the structural carcass of the composition would be left. This aspect of some of the later work of Rimsky-Korsakov and Tchaikovsky should never be overlooked when antecedents are being sought for Stravinsky's native talent for thinking himself right into the instrumental colouring in his music.

That *The Sleeping Beauty* is Tchaikovsky's masterpiece of ballet music is such a generally acknowledged fact that it hardly needs to be repeated. From the point of view of pure lyrical beauty it could be argued that *Swan Lake* is superior. But as ballet music *per se The Sleeping Beauty* is even more original.[17] Its masterly originality was not really understood by the first audiences, despite the lavishness of the production and the superb choreography of Marius Petipa. Tchaikovsky was hurt by the Tsar's attitude after the gala rehearsal in St Petersburg on 2/14 January 1890, the day before the first public performance. 'His majesty treated me with distant hauteur',[18] he noted in his diary.

Tchaikovsky had been appointed a director of the Russian Musical Society some years earlier, and in this capacity he became a member of the committee formed to arrange the anniversary celebrations commemorating the fiftieth year since Anton Rubinstein made his début as a pianist in 1839. He contributed two compositions, an *a cappella* chorus entitled *Greeting to A. G. Rubinstein*, performed on 18/30 November 1889, and an *Impromptu* in A♭ major which was included in an album of piano music composed by former pupils and presented to Rubinstein on the same evening. On the next two consecutive days Tchaikovsky conducted two programmes of Rubin-

[16] RN, p. 426.
[17] See Chapter 12, pp. 140–1.
[18] RN, p. 482.

stein's works. His feelings on the subject were revealed to Mme von Meck, to whom he confided that he 'wondered how he endured it'. Three years earlier he had written in the private pages of his diary: 'Played over [Rubinstein's opera] *Nero*. My amazement can know no bounds at the brazen off-handedness of the composer. Oh! you buffoon. Good God, it makes me furious to look through this score ... You think your own writing is vile, then you look at this rubbish, which was nevertheless performed seriously, and your soul feels lighter.'[19]

While in Petersburg for the rehearsals of *The Sleeping Beauty* he took the opportunity of discussing with Vsevolozhsky and the Theatre Directorate an unfinished libretto on *The Queen of Spades* which Modest had originally been preparing for N. S. Klenovsky. Klenovsky willingly abandoned his claim to Modest's sentimental travesty of Pushkin's original tale. Vsevolozhsky was keen on the idea, especially as the opera would prove a suitable vehicle to display the talent of the popular tenor Nicholas Figner and his wife Medea. The libretto with various changes was approved by the Director and soon after the first performance of *The Sleeping Beauty* Tchaikovsky left for Florence, where he started work on the opera on 19/31 January 1890.

[19] *ibid.*, p. 364; RG and EV, 1/13 March 1886.

11

The last years 2 (1890–3)

The libretto of *The Queen of Spades* still needed to be cut, and other alterations were necessary; Tchaikovsky made some of these himself. The basic plot is concerned with the twofold subject of love and gambling. Hermann loves Liza, who returns his love but is betrothed to another. Hermann, fascinated by gambling, learns that Liza's guardian, the old Countess, knows the secret of an infallible winning sequence of three cards. Introduced clandestinely to her bedroom, he tries to extract the secret of the three cards from her and frightens her literally to death. In a later scene her ghost tells him the secret: 'Three, seven, ace'. When it becomes clear to Liza, after a rendezvous with Hermann by the canal opposite the Winter Palace, that his mania for cards is more powerful than his love, she throws herself into the canal. The final scene of the opera is a gambling club where Hermann wins twice and then loses all on the Queen of Spades, which he has played by some unaccountable mistake instead of the ace. The frustrated lover and compulsive gambler are combined in one unfortunate person who, after his colossal gambling loss, pauses only for the space of a soft melodramatic *arioso*, heard above the ghostly Countess's descending whole-tone scale, before thrusting a dagger into his own heart. Thus the equally suicidal hero and heroine never consummate their love and the old Countess, the Queen of Spades herself, takes her revenge.

The close is very different in Pushkin, where neither of the two principals die, by their own or anybody else's hand; but in the sophisticated eyes of the poet himself and his original aristocratic readers each suffers a fate worse than death: while Hermann ends up in a lunatic asylum rapidly and endlessly muttering the words: 'Three, seven, ace! Three, seven, Queen', Liza marries a proper young man in the Civil Service, 'the son of the old Countess's former steward'. Such an end would not have done at all for Tchaikovsky who was unable to appreciate this sort of irony, far less depict it in his music. As it was, the idea of an evil old woman who personifies 'Fate' and is responsible for the ruin of a love-affair, and the consequent acting out

by both lovers of their suicidal tendencies, was one which greatly
appealed to him. An additional factor in his success in identifying
himself with Hermann was that he was writing the part for Figner,
with whom he was in complete sympathy. Liza, too, who sees the
light of love in Hermann's eye replaced by the glitter of the mad
gambler, was a character for whom Tchaikovsky could really feel
passionately.

It is this personal commitment on the part of the composer that is
the prime factor in the overall success of *The Queen of Spades*. But it
is worth while examining some of the other elements which contribute
to that success, in spite of the opera's moments of conventionality and
tawdry theatricality, which include the occasional climactic use of that
hackneyed old war-horse the diminished seventh – by this time not
quite at the end of its long career as a purveyor of evil. There are
many moments of superb lyricism and dramatic power. Liza's aria of
sorrow as she waits for her lover by the canal in the penultimate scene
is a good example of the typical Glinka-type aria. In this case it is
derived from the aria 'They guess the truth' which Susannin sings in
Act IV of *A Life for the Tsar* when he realizes that he must perish.
Compare the melodic and rhythmic shape of this aria (Ex. 18(a)) with
Tchaikovsky's (Ex. 18(b)):

Ex. 18

Tchaikovsky returns to Glinka to be inspired with a greater simplicity, directness and immediacy of utterance. Another important
aspect of his late style to be found in *The Queen of Spades* is his ability
to develop dramatic situations symphonically, and to offset the points
of high drama with contrasting material which seems to enhance their
power. There are examples of this throughout, as in the scene in the
Countess's bedroom: before she is frightened to death by Hermann,
thinking herself alone, she croons a Grétry air popular in the time of

her youth. All the pseudo-rococo insets in the opera have this effect of highlighting the action with which they are juxtaposed.

The drama is certainly advanced in the ballroom scene, at the beginning of Act II, by the depiction in various ways of the increasing absorption of Hermann with the three-card story; but the whole scene, with its pseudo-Mozartian introduction and opening chorus, its final polonaise and its 'Faithful shepherdess' rococo interlude, is relaxed in comparison with the scene in Liza's room which precedes it and the crucial scene in the Countess's bedroom which follows. It is all carefully thought out in these terms, so that not only each separate scene but the entire opera is developed satisfactorily. In one sense the 'Faithful shepherdess' interlude can even be considered as the central obverse of the main plot of the opera. For the shepherdess, eschewing her rich lover, chooses the poor shepherd with whom she is in love, and in the final chorus of the interlude it is made quite clear that their love will be consummated – a make-believe happy ending which is in contradistinction to the reality of the sad fate of Hermann and Liza.

Tchaikovsky's favourite downward-scale type of melody took on additional significance in *The Queen of Spades*. Here it signifies not Fate's cruelty resulting in the unhappy outcome of true love, as in *Eugene Onegin*, but Fate's cruelty resulting in Death. After the exit of the Countess near the end of the scene in Liza's room, Hermann finishes a phrase, in which he commands Death to be gone, with a downward scale that is repeated sequentially by the full orchestra *fortissimo*. The three cards which cause death are first referred to – in Scene I – as follows:

Ex. 19

tri kar - ty, tri kar-ty, tri kar-ty,

The last three notes of that phrase are derived from the opera's frequently recurring motto-theme (not unlike that of *Eugene Onegin*).

Tchaikovsky worked speedily on *The Queen of Spades*. He had finished the vocal score by 26 March/7 April. This speed was necessary for the opera to be ready for 'next season', as had been planned, but he found the work went easily and he told Modest that he thought it was his masterpiece.[1] He did not return to Russia until 22 April/4 May. The full score was finished on 8/20 June.

While still in Italy he had had the idea of writing a string sextet. After the successful completion of *The Queen of Spades* he set to work on it with a joyful heart. Although he found it difficult to write for six independent voices of equal timbre, as he wrote to Modest,[2] he had finished the rough draft within seventeen days: 'For the present I'm awfully pleased with it.'[3] But before its first performance two years later at a concert of the Petersburg Chamber Music Society, he revised it completely, giving it the subtitle *Souvenir de Florence*. The subtitle is slightly misleading, since the only things about the work that are really Italianate are the superbly lyrical melodies and the predominantly sunny nature of the music, in spite of a tonic key in the minor mode. Tchaikovsky exhibits his Russian nationality to the full as always in his best compositions; but there is a certain thoroughly absorbed German influence all the same, especially in the first movement. Colin Mason has pointed out a similarity to Brahms 'in the frequent use of the second violin and violas in moving, but purely harmonic passages, identically figured, creating a unifying inner web'.[4] Another Teutonically inspired feature (but not carried out in a Teutonic manner) is the superb contrapuntal interweaving of the galaxy of themes in the development section. Tchaikovsky is as masterly here as he is feeble in the fugue of the First Suite, curiously enough in the same key of D minor. The third movement consists entirely of Russian folk-like material. Perhaps the most strikingly original effect is in the *Moderato* middle section of the second movement. Here the strings play block chords reiterated in semiquaver triplets *a punta d'arco*, with many and sudden variations in volume and no trace of any theme – an essay in pure sound.

After a round of visits during the summer Tchaikovsky finished up in the autumn with Anatol in Tiflis. It was here that a totally unexpected letter from Mme von Meck was responsible for the permanent destruction of his happiness. In it she told him that she was on the verge of financial ruin and could no longer continue his annuity. 'Good-bye, my dear, incomparable friend', she concluded, 'and do not forget one whose love for you is infinite'.[5] This was a bitter blow to

[1] RL, p. 451.
[2] *ibid.*, p. 462.
[3] *ibid.*, p. 465.
[4] ER (5), pp. 111–12.
[5] RK, Vol. III, p. 604.

Tchaikovsky's pride. Worried though he was about the financial aspect of the matter, he was far more hurt that she took it for granted that the discontinuance of his dependence on her financial assistance would automatically mean the permanent rupture of their friendship. He immediately replied that it would make no difference, but she did not answer. He soon learnt that there was nothing wrong with her financial affairs. As a matter of fact he was shortly to become better off financially than he had ever been. The von Meck pension accounted for only about one-third of his total income, and the enormous success of *The Queen of Spades* after its first performance in 7/19 December, together with the continuing success of *Eugene Onegin*, provided royalties which more than made up the loss.

What he could not endure was the ever-recurring thought that he had, after all, been the mere plaything of a rich woman whose gifts of money had given her a kind of claim on him – a claim which, as would have been the case with one of the musicians she employed, she had immediately to relinquish with her cessation of his 'salary'. He had considered their relationship to have transcended this sort of thing, and her action shattered his faith in human nature. It is very doubtful if he was right in his suspicions, but even had he known the full facts he was probably too egocentric to have been able to see the affair from any other viewpoint than his own. Mme von Meck had been mentally and physically ill for a number of years. Her recurrent cough seems to point to tuberculosis, and her complete absorption in her family to that very misanthropy and agoraphobia which Tchaikovsky himself had by now so successfully thrown off. Her eldest son Vladimir had become a mental and physical wreck and was wasting away before her eyes. It is not improbable that she developed an overpowering guilt-complex, blaming herself for bestowing love and money upon an outsider which should have been exclusively reserved for her son and the other members of the family.[6] It was her duty to break off the relationship, and she did not trust herself to re-open the correspondence. Vladimir was to live for only another eighteen months, by which time his mother was also far gone. She outlived Tchaikovsky by only a few months.

[6]In addition, according to the von Meck family, she was being blackmailed by her son-in-law, Prince Shirinsky-Shikhmatov, over the illegitimacy of his wife, Mme von Meck's daughter Milochka. Also, according to Galina von Meck, there was a reconciliation between her grandmother and great-uncle in 1893: see Edward Garden's Introduction to *To my best friend: Correspondence between Tchaikovsky and Nadezhda von Meck, 1876–78* (Oxford, 1993), p. xxxv.

The first time Tchaikovsky mentioned his work on the composition of the Symphonic Ballad *The Voyevoda* (nothing to do with his earlier opera of the same name) was on 28 September/10 October, six days after he had received the devastating shock which resulted from Mme von Meck's final letter. It is not surprising, in consequence, that this work freezes one to the very marrow of the bone, and contains quite the most spine-chilling music Tchaikovsky ever produced. As usual, he had in mind the orchestration while composing it. A week or so later he told Bob Davydov that he had finished the short score: 'I want to devote all next week to its instrumentation. I assure you that it was indeed a brainwave to write this composition.' However, he clearly needed a great deal more time to mull over the orchestration, which was not written down for nearly a year. As a result of the success of *The Queen of Spades* the Directorate of the Imperial Theatres commissioned a one-act opera and a ballet for the following season. But before he started on either of these, at the request of the actor Lucien Guitry he wrote some incidental music for *Hamlet*, drawing on his *Snow Maiden* music and the second movement of his Third Symphony and using a re-orchestrated and cut version of his overture-fantasia for the overture. Only the introduction to Act V, also used later as the funeral march, was newly composed.

It was at this time that Tchaikovsky became very friendly with the group of composers who had been befriended by M. P. Belyaev. This millionaire timber merchant paid for the publication and performance of the works of certain Russian composers, including Rimsky-Korsakov. Balakirev could not stand Belyaev, but Tchaikovsky could hardly have been aware that he was setting the seal on his estrangement with Balakirev by mixing with the Belyaev circle. He enjoyed their company and according to Rimsky-Korsakov sat around in restaurants with them 'till about three in the morning'. Tchaikovsky could drink 'a great deal of wine' while still keeping command of 'all his faculties, physical and mental; very few were able to keep up with him in this respect'.[7] Rimsky-Korsakov states that Tchaikovsky's old friend Laroche began to appear more and more at the gatherings. He himself disliked Laroche and did all he could to avoid him. However, it is unlikely that Tchaikovsky knew about Rimsky-Korsakov's dislike of Laroche any more than he knew about Balakirev's dislike of Belyaev.[8] These little Petersburg animosities were no doubt beyond a mere Muscovite.

[7] RD, p. 269.
[8] In 1891 Rimsky-Korsakov and Balakirev were not on speaking terms either.

121

Tchaikovsky had asked Modest to prepare a libretto based on the Danish poet Herz's play *King René's Daughter*, which he renamed *Iolanta*. Meanwhile he started work on a ballet forced on him by Petipa and the Theatre Directorate, based on E.T.A. Hoffmann's tale *Nutcracker and the Mouse King*. He wrote to Modest on 25 February/9 March: 'I'm working extremely hard and I'm beginning to reconcile myself to the subject of the ballet'.[9] In April he was to fulfil a long-felt desire to go on a conducting tour of the United States. Composition of *Nutcracker* continued in Berlin and Paris, where he was extremely homesick. Just before he was due to sail for America, Modest heard of Sasha's death and tried to keep it from his brother.[10] But he read of it in a newspaper and set sail in a black mood. He was very worried about the effect the death of his sister would have on her son Bob. At this of all times he was trying to conjure up suitable music to portray the sugar-plum fairy, which he found 'absolutely impossible'.[11]

He had been invited to New York by Walter Damrosch to conduct at the opening festival concerts of the Music Hall, the original name for the Carnegie Hall. He also conducted concerts in Philadelphia and Baltimore and visited Niagara Falls and Washington. His four concerts in New York were triumphantly successful: after the First Piano Concerto 'the enthusiasm was greater than anything I've experienced, even in Russia', as he confided in the very full diary he kept of his American trip. He liked the warm-hearted Americans but disliked the critics' habit of devoting so much space to personal appearance and stance at the rostrum. But he was amused at the following description of him in the *New York Herald* of 6 May (24 April), which he quotes in his diary: 'Tchaikovsky is a tall, gray, well-built, interesting man *well on to sixty*(?!!)'.[12] He was actually one day short of fifty-one. He enjoyed the food and drink, especially 'some kind of mixture of *whisky, bitters* and *lemon* – extraordinarily delicious'. He continued for the rest of his life to consume prodigious quantities of food and drink and to suffer from indigestion; but his eating and drinking habits did not have one result that might have been expected, since his expenditure of nervous energy insured him against the acquisition of anything much in the way of a paunch.

As a result of the success of his American tour he arrived back in Europe in a much happier frame of mind. At the beginning of June

[9]RL, p. 476.
[10]RH, Vol. III, p. 433 *et seq.*
[11]RL, pp. 480–1.
[12]EV, 6 May 1891 (and RG).

he returned not to Frolovskoye, where all the beautiful surrounding woods had been cut down, but to his old house at Maidanovo. On 3/15 June he wrote to Jurgenson asking him to order a new instrument he had heard in Paris, as he wanted to use it before Rimsky-Korsakov and Glazunov got wind of it – the celesta, with its 'divinely beautiful tone'.[13] He had finished the sketch of *Nutcracker* by 24 June/6 July, including the 'Dance of the Suger-Plum Fairy' in which the icing-sugary effect of the celesta is so much better known than its much more remarkable icily chilling effect in *The Voyevoda* – not to be orchestrated for another three months. On the next day he told Bob that *Nutcracker* was 'incomparably inferior to *The Sleeping Beauty* – I'm in no doubt about this'.[14] For once Tchaikovsky was right: the wedding-cake charm of *Nutcracker* has a defect for which it is impossible to excuse Tchaikovsky – it is bogus. The icing is made from saccharine and the cake itself from *ersatz* ingredients.

The same is unfortunately true of the one-act opera on which he immediately started work, although he warmed to the subject of *Iolanta*. When he had finished the short score, before starting the orchestration, he scored instead the Symphonic Ballad *The Voyevoda*, which portrays his real feelings at the time – approximately one year after the sheet-anchor of his storm-tossed emotional life had been removed. His sombre mood even overflows occasionally into the predominantly superficial *Iolanta*, as in the dark colouring of the short orchestral introduction, perhaps suggesting Iolanta's blindness, and the taut emotional world of the Sixth Symphony is anticipated here and there. But the eighteenth-century type of theme played by the orchestra at the beginning of Scene I is suspiciously like the well-known minuet from Handel's *Berenice* – a curiously anachronistic way to evoke an atmosphere of fifteenth-century Provence; the music employed when the blind Iolanta receives her sight is trite; and nothing could be feebler than this musical *réchauffé* which occurs in the big duet between Iolanta and the hero Vaudemont (see Ex. 20). The music which inspired this was undoubtedly the delicate passage for Antonida and Sobinin from the trio in Act I of Glinka's *A Life for the Tsar* (see Ex. 21). Tchaikovsky had already made much better use of this material at the beginning of the 'Providence' motive in the Fifth Symphony.

[13] RJ, Vol. II, p. 212.
[14] RL, pp. 494–5.

Tchaikovsky

Ex. 20

ff Chud-ny per - ve-nets tvo-re - nya,

per - vy mi - ru dar tvor-tsa

Ex. 21

Ne svo-di - na go - re

It is obvious why *Iolanta* does not ring true. The heroine's blindness is cured through the love of the hero, and the two live happily ever after. How could Tchaikovsky identify himself with such a heroine, with such ideally consummated love? For him the world of opera was very real, but such an ending was outside the bounds of his experience. Only when it could be allotted to a former world of idealized bliss seen through rose-tinted spectacles, as in the pastoral interlude in *The Queen of Spades*, could the apparent falseness of a happy ending such as this be cancelled out by the intensely felt stilted nature of the musical semi-pastiche. Even in *The Sleeping Beauty* a chill is cast over the blissful realm of fantasy after the general rejoicing in the final mazurka, when a sudden austere change to the minor mode serves to jerk us back from the rarefied fairy-tale atmosphere towards the very different world of real life. Rimsky-Korsakov's opinions were often one-sided, but it is difficult to disagree with him that *Iolanta* is 'one of Tchaikovsky's feeblest compositions.'[15]

Tchaikovsky conducted the first performance of the Symphonic Ballad *The Voyevoda* at a concert in Moscow on 6/18 November which also included a performance of Grieg's Piano Concerto with A. I. Siloti as soloist. He told Anatol: 'There was fervent applause. As the new piece *The Voyevoda* proved to be basically very unsuccessful, I'm going to destroy it. I fear that this is an indication of the decline of my powers, although Taneyev has high praise for the new opera [*Iolanta*], which he's arranging for piano.'[16] The general public had given an enthusiastic reception to *The Voyevoda*, but at the rehearsal the orchestral players had clearly not liked it. In the creative afterglow of the opera and the orchestral piece Tchaikovsky's own instinctive feelings were subordinated to the opinions of the players and Taneyev. His subconscious originality had outstripped his powers of conscious criticism. He destroyed the full score of *The Voyevoda*, but Siloti preserved the orchestral parts and it was reconstructed from these and published after Tchaikovsky's death. Tchaikovsky temporarily misunderstood the course of his own development. The result was a backward step in his next work, an abortive Symphony in E♭ major. But this was succeeded by the composition in which he took by far the greatest stride forward of his career: the Symphony in B minor (eventually No. 6). He was certainly convinced that he was at the

---

[15] RD, p. 284.
[16] RL, p. 504.

height of his powers in this, the crowning achievement of his life's work.

At the end of December he set out on another tour, conducting his works in Kiev and Warsaw before arriving at Hamburg to direct *Eugene Onegin*, which was to be performed in German. At the rehearsal he was unable to cope with the changes necessitated by the translation from Russian to German, and he refused to conduct the performance. He wrote to Bob on 7/19 January, 1892:

> By the way the *Kapellmeister* here is not a mediocre nobody, but a versatile genius who is consumed with desire to conduct the first performance. Yesterday I heard under his direction a *most wonderful* performance of *Tannhäuser*. The singers, the orchestra, Pollini,[17] the producers and stage-managers, the *Kapellmeister* (his surname is Mahler) have all fallen in love with *Eugene Onegin*.[18]

The next day he told Anatol: 'As far as the music was concerned the performance [conducted by Mahler] was magnificent ... it was a considerable success.'[19] Arrived in Paris, he felt overpoweringly home-sick, and failed to be amused by a visit to the Folies-Bergère. 'This is a sort of colossal *café-chantant*', he told Bob. 'I was bored stiff. The Russian clown Durov presented 230 trained rats ... It's curious how the Parisians demonstrate their philo-Russianism. They're not giving a single Russian concert, opera or play.'[20] After ten days in Paris he returned home, cancelling some concerts he was to have given in the Netherlands.

At Maidanovo he orchestrated some of the best numbers from his new ballet and made them into a suite. Neither *Nutcracker* nor *Iolanta* was due to receive its first performance until the end of the year, but he was to have conducted the first Petersburg performance of *The Voyevoda* on 7/19 March, and this suite from *Nutcracker* was expeditiously put together so that he could present something new in its stead. The substitution could hardly have presented a greater contrast. But the citizens of the freezing northern capital, still in the depths of winter in early March, certainly enjoyed the tinselly warmth of the *Nutcracker* Suite more than they would have enjoyed the chill depths of *The Voyevoda*. They encored every number but one.

On 5/17 May Tchaikovsky moved into a new house on the outskirts

---

[17]B. Pollini (1838–97), director of the Hamburg Opera.
[18]RL, p. 506.
[19]*ibid.*, p. 507.
[20]*ibid.*, p. 508.

of Klin itself. (This house, restored after its devastation during the Nazi invasion, is now the Tchaikovsky Museum.) Here he started the new symphony (in E♭ major), but the strain of overwork was beginning to tell and he was advised to take the cure at Vichy. He spent three weeks there with Bob. On his return to Russia he worked 'assiduously' on the rough short score of the symphony and all but completed it. However by the end of the year he told Bob that he had not orchestrated it and that it had got stuck. He had written it for the sake of writing: 'There is nothing in the least interesting or attractive in it. I've decided to throw it out and forget about it. I'm delighted to have come to this irrevocable decision.'[21] But as usual he was disinclined to waste material, and he arranged the first movement of the discarded symphony as a concert piece for piano and orchestra the next summer, and the *Andante* and finale were similarly arranged but were left in short score with no indication that they were destined to be joined with the other movement as a concerto.

The première of the double bill consisting of *Iolanta* and *Nutcracker* on 6/18 December was only partially successful. The public clearly did not like the ballet in spite of its sumptuous production. But the Tsar, present at the dress rehearsal, had liked *Iolanta* and the public agreed with him. It remained popular during the nineties. A week after this double première Tchaikovsky once again travelled abroad. He was to conduct a concert of his works in Brussels at the beginning of January, but he went first to Basle en route to Montbeillard, where he had discovered that his old governess Fanny Dürbach was living. 'Mlle Fanny' did not know Modest or Anatol, so he wrote about her first to Nicholas:

Although she is now 70, *she is little changed* ... I was very much afraid that there would be tears and a scene, but nothing of the sort transpired. She greeted me as though it was only a year since we'd seen each other – with joy, tenderness and great simplicity ... Subsequently she showed me *our exercise books* ... my work, your and my letters, but, most interesting of all, some wonderfully dear letters of Mama ... I seemed to breathe the air of our Votkinsk home and hear the voice of Mama and the others. She gave me as a present one wonderful letter from Mama.[22]

The concert in Brussels was well received by the public, but was not such a triumphant success as a series of concerts he conducted in

[21] RL, p. 523.
[22] *ibid.*, pp. 526–7.

Odessa on his return to Russia.[23] It was in Odessa that Kuznetsov painted his well-known portrait (see illustration) which Modest considered to be the most 'living' picture of his brother in existence. It shows a deep-thinking, rather care-worn but not humourless white-haired man who might be a well-preserved sixty-five. With Tchaikovsky, not yet fifty-three, the ageing process was accelerating to an almost alarming degree, as he filled his life more and more with feverish activity. But he arrived back home at the beginning of February well satisfied with his recent tour.

[23] RH, Vol. III, pp. 595–8.

12

Sixth Symphony, Death and Posthumous Influence

By the last year of his life Tchaikovsky had achieved a success given to few composers during their lifetime. His compositions were played to enthusiastic audiences all over Europe and America. His music was fashionable. He was in constant demand as a conductor. Honours began to come to him. He was elected a corresponding member of the Académie Française. C. V. Stanford wrote on behalf of Cambridge University offering him an honorary doctorate of music there, together with Saint-Saëns, Boito, Bruch and Grieg. He accepted.

He was not due in England until the end of May (N.S.). In the meantime, back in Klin after his triumphs in Odessa, he started work on his Sixth Symphony. On 11/23 February 1893 he wrote to Bob Davydov:

> During my travels I had an idea for another symphony, this time a programme-symphony, but with a programme which shall remain a mystery for every one – let them guess away, but the symphony will be called merely *A Programme Symphony* (No. 6). The programme itself is subjective to the core ... As regards form there will be in this symphony a great deal that is new, and among other things the finale will be, not a noisy *Allegro* but, on the contrary, a very leisurely *Adagio*. You can't conceive what bliss it is to be convinced that my time is not yet over and that I'm still able to work.[1]

But concerts in Moscow and Kharkov interrupted work on the symphony, which was not resumed until 19/31 March. Five days later it was finished.[2] Tchaikovsky did not proceed directly to its instrumentation. As was now his custom, he let his ideas for the orchestral colour ripen in his mind and proceeded to compose something else – in this case, the eighteen pieces for piano, Op. 72, and the six songs, Op. 73. He told Bob that the piano pieces were 'mediocre'. 'I've no desire at all to compose them, but am doing so for money. All I'm

[1]RL, p. 532.
[2]RH, Vol. III, p. 656.

trying for is that they shan't turn out too badly.'[3] Weak though most of them are, with titles such as 'Un poco di Chopin' and 'Un poco di Schumann', 'Écho rustique' and the like, one piece is of particular interest, not for its content, which is indeed 'mediocre', but for its title: 'Valse à cinq temps'. Composed so soon after the short score of the Sixth Symphony, this 'Valse' with five beats in a bar was clearly composed in the wake of the second movement of the Sixth Symphony, which can on this evidence certainly be confidently called a five-four Valse, since Tchaikovsky himself was clearly thinking of it as such.

The songs are of a very much higher calibre, perhaps because they were dedicated to the 'sympathetic' Figner. Particularly good is the last one in the group, 'Again, as before, alone'. The stark emotional atmosphere is vividly portrayed by the music with its very simple repetitive inward-turning melody and semitonally descending appoggiaturas in the accompaniment. This is all in the same world as *The Queen of Spades*, but in its terseness and simplicity it is perhaps more advanced and typical of Tchaikovsky's very last period. It certainly gives us a fascinating glimpse of the kind of music which might have been found in Tchaikovsky's next opera, had he lived to compose it. He had been trying to find a suitable libretto but had dismissed Modest's suggestion of the Hindu legend *Nal and Damayanti*[4] because it was 'too far removed from life'. He wanted something resembling *Carmen* or Mascagni's *Cavalleria Rusticana* (first produced three years earlier).

He arrived in 'ugly' London on 17/29 May and conducted his Fourth Symphony at a Royal Philharmonic Society concert three days later.[5] He informed Modest that 'the concert was a brilliant success, i.e., the unanimous opinion was that I had a veritable triumph, so that Saint-Saëns, who appeared after me, suffered a little because of my extraordinary success'.[6] All the future doctors were in London except the ailing Grieg. Besides Saint-Saëns only Boito attracted him. As for Bruch, he was a 'sickeningly arrogant' person.[7] The degrees were awarded in Cambridge on 1/13 June. A concert had taken place there the day before at which music by all the honorary doctors was performed. Tchaikovsky conducted *Francesca da Rimini*. Cambridge, 'with its *colleges* resembling monasteries and its peculiar customs and

[3] RL, p. 535.
[4] Arensky later composed an opera on this subject.
[5] RN, p. 583.
[6] RL, p. 540
[7] *ibid.*, p. 541.

traditions which retain much from mediaeval times,' created a 'very favourable impression'.[8]

On his return to Russia, after visits to Modest at Grankino and Nicholas at Ukolovo, he started work on the orchestration of the Sixth Symphony at Klin on 20 July/1 August. 'The further I get with the instrumentation, the more difficulty it causes me', he told Modest two days later. 'Twenty years ago I rushed along at full speed without giving it a thought, and it turned out well. Now I've become timid, unsure of myself. Today I spent the entire day sitting over two pages; nothing really turns out as I'd like it to. But the work is progressing all the same.'[9] He was still having difficulty with it nearly a fortnight later, but he wrote to Bob that he definitely considered it to be the best, the *'most sincere'* of all his works. 'I love it as I've never loved a single one of my other musical progeny.'[10] He told Jurgenson the same, writing to him on 12/24 August that the orchestration had at last been completed.[11] He wrote to Anatol the same day that the comparative slowness of his orchestration had not been caused by a deterioration in his powers, but was a result of 'my having become a great deal stricter with myself ... I'm very proud of the symphony, and I think that it is the best of my compositions'.

He was so elated by his work on the symphony that not even the deaths of his former colleague Albrecht, his old school friend the poet Apukhtin and Vladimir Shilovsky could depress him. The Grand Duke Constantine suggested that he should compose a setting of Apukhtin's *The Requiem*, but he declined on the grounds that 'my last symphony (especially the finale) is permeated with a similar mood'.[12] He conducted the première of the symphony in St Petersburg on 16/28 October. He had been a little dispirited during the rehearsals by the lack of enthusiasm of the orchestral players, and the symphony was received by the public in the politely restrained Petersburg manner – very different from the ovations to which he had recently been treated in Kharkov, Odessa and even London. The press was on the whole favourable, and one notice supplemented its praise by stating that if it had been conducted by Auer or Nápravník it would have achieved greater success. But Rimsky-Korsakov disagreed with that, declaring in his autobiography that Tchaikovsky's performance had been excellent.

[8] RJ, Vol. II, p. 263.
[9] RL, p. 546.
[10] *ibid.*, p. 547.
[11] RJ, Vol. II, p. 269.
[12] RN, p. 592.

On the morning after the première Modest found his brother trying to decide on a title. He now felt that it was not satisfactory to call it a 'Programme Symphony' without giving it a programme, but he did not want to give it simply a number. Modest's suggestion of 'Tragic' did not please him. 'I went out of the room still leaving Peter Ilyich undecided. Then there suddenly came into my head the title "pathétique". I returned, and, I remember as if it were yesterday, standing in the doorway, I uttered this word. "Excellent, Modya, bravo, *pathéthique*".'[13] The next day (18/30 October) Tchaikovsky wrote to Jurgenson that the symphony was 'not disliked, but has caused some bewilderment. I myself am prouder of it than of any of my other compositions'.[14]

According to Modest, in his biography of his brother,[15] three days after writing this letter he complained of insomnia and 'indigestion'. He had been sitting drinking until two in the morning at a restaurant the previous evening. He thought it was his usual 'stomach cramps' and refused to send for a doctor. He sat down at the luncheon table with Modest and Bob. He was unable to eat anything but drank a glass of unboiled water in spite of their warnings about the dangers of cholera. By evening his condition was so much worse that Modest sent for the brothers Lev and Vasily Bertenson, two of the best doctors in St Petersburg, who diagnosed cholera. Only once in the painful course of the disease was there a momentary hope for his life. Several times he said: 'I believe it's death'.

Alexandra Orlova tells a very different story.[16] Not only do Modest's and Lev Bertenson's published versions of the course of his 'illness' differ in important respects, but the usual sanitary precautions were not taken at Modest's flat, where Tchaikovsky was staying. After his death many people came to the flat to pay their respects. It is perhaps unlikely that this would have been allowed had he died of cholera, according to Mrs Orlova. And Rimsky-Korsakov remarked in his autobiography, 'How strange that, though death resulted from cholera, nevertheless admission to the requiems was unrestricted. I recall that Verzhbilovich [a professor of cello at the Petersburg Conservatoire] kissed the body on the head and face'.[17] Mrs Orlova's late husband,

[13] RH, Vol. III, pp. 644–5.
[14] RJ, Vol. II, p. 273.
[15] Illness and death of Tchaikovsky: RH, Vol. III, pp. 648–54.
[16] Alexandra Orlova (trans. David Brown), 'Tchaikovsky: The Last Chapter' in *Music & Letters*, April 1981, Vol. 62 No. 2, pp. 125–45.
[17] RD, p. 298.

Georgy Orlov, was apparently told by Dr Vasily Bertenson himself, shortly before his death in 1933, that Tchaikovsky had poisoned himself. In her article, Mrs Orlova also reveals an account of how this was alleged to have come about, dictated to her in 1966 by Alexander Voitov of the Russian Museum in Leningrad (as it then was). Like Tchaikovsky (though much later, of course), Voitov had been a pupil at the School of Jurisprudence and had collected biographical materials on many of the school's former pupils. According to Voitov, Duke Stenbok-Fermor wrote a letter to Alexander III complaining of 'the attention which the composer was paying his young nephew' and gave the letter to the senior procurator of the Senate, Nikolay Jacobi (who had been a contemporary of Tchaikovsky at the school), to pass to the Tsar. Afraid of the dishonour that exposure would bring on the school and its old boys, Jacobi set up a 'court of honour' consisting of himself and six other former school friends of Tchaikovsky, who was summoned to appear before the 'court' on 19/31 October. To avoid scandal, 'they required him to kill himself'. The poison for the purpose (possibly arsenic) may have been delivered to Tchaikovsky on the next morning by the barrister Auguste Gerke, another old boy of the school; the ostensible reason for Gerke's visit was to take Tchaikovsky an agreement with the publishing firm of Bessel concerning his opera *The Oprichnik*. This visit was reported by Vasily Bessel in *Russkaya muzykalnaya gazeta*, 1897, No. 12, but was omitted by Modest in his account. As a result of taking the poison, Tchaikovsky suffered appalling agony. He died in the early morning of 25 October/6 November.

Mrs Orlova's version has been strenuously refuted by Alexander Poznansky,[18] who rightly states that many leading figures in Russia at this time were homosexuals, and that their homosexuality was well-known. However, this does not necessarily negate Mrs Orlova's version, since in such cases a periodic clamp-down was seen as necessary if things were getting out of hand to too great an extent – a case in point is the treatment of Oscar Wilde in England in the same decade; in England, as in Russia, a number of prominent men at the time were homosexuals. This did not prevent Wilde's disgrace and imprisonment. Nevertheless, Poznansky does make a case against the suicide theory; it is enough to say here that, unless more material

[18] Alexander Poznansky, (trans. Ralph C. Burr, Jr.), 'Tchaikovsky's Suicide: Myth and Reality' in *19th Century Music*, Spring 1988, Vol. II No. 3, pp. 199–220.

becomes available from the Tchaikovsky Museum at Klin, the case for or against suicide must remain unproven.

On 29 October/10 November, after a magnificent funeral service in the Kazan Cathedral, he was buried in the cemetery of the Alexander-Nevsky monastery, not far from the graves of Glinka, Borodin and Mussorgsky. Balakirev outlived him by nearly seventeen years, Rimsky-Korsakov by fifteen, and even old Stassov had another thirteen years to live.

His death shocked the musical world. On 6/18 November Nápravník conducted the Sixth Symphony at a concert in his memory. We know that he considered the last movement to be about 'death' and in the nature of a 'requiem'. The audience at the concert were deeply moved and the *Adagio lamentoso* finale was now proclaimed to be 'prophetic'. Even in these early days, rumours were rife about Tchaikovsky's suicide and these did the success of the symphony no harm, even if they were not entirely responsible for the instant fame it achieved. It was not long before it had been performed with triumphant success all over Europe and in America. It had a profound influence upon European musical consciousness, especially in Germany and Austria, and so famous did Tchaikovsky become in the 1890s that a few of the obituaries of Brahms in 1897 were perhaps not as totally eulogistic as they might otherwise have been. This would hardly be worth mentioning – since it has nothing to do with the relative merit of the music of the two composers – were it not for the fact that it may possibly have had some bearing on their posthumous influence. With the exception of a peripheral influence upon a composer like Schoenberg, Brahms's influence was mostly on minor composers, for example Dohnanyi; and steeped though Brahms's music was in the central European tradition, it was the 'barbarous' Russian composer who was to have much the greater influence upon that tradition, as well as reconciling his national folk idiom with the mainstream of European music. This does not make him a 'cosmopolitan' composer, any more than Bartók, who also achieved this reconciliation, is 'cosmopolitan'.

It would require far more space than is available in this volume to examine the influence of Tchaikovsky's music in detail. Before making a few comments on the subject, it will be well to inspect more closely the single work that was most immediately influential – the Sixth Symphony in B minor. The instrumentation is of paramount importance from the very first bar of the *Adagio* introduction. A low bassoon solo over *divisi* double basses, soon joined by *divisi* violas, foreshadows the first subject of the *Allegro non troppo*, which seems to express the struggles involved in the upward thrust for life. In the introduction, however, it soon sinks back into the depths in a descending scale which can be thought of as the motto-theme of death itself:

Ex. 22

Tovey has remarked: 'All Tchaikovsky's music is dramatic; and the Pathetic Symphony is the most dramatic of all his works.'[19] Martin Cooper has been more specific in citing examples of certain operatic prototypes of the music of the *Allegro non troppo*. For example, he compares Tchaikovsky's figuration especially at the *poco più animato*[20] with 'the long solo passage [in the final bedchamber scene of Verdi's *Otello*] for the double basses punctuated by staccato semiquavers in the violas and the persistent recurrence of the staccato figure in the basses, followed ... by a single "note of doom" in the brass'.[21]

The undercurrents and occasional eruptions of violence in the concise four-square first subject are almost viciously contrasted with the *Andante* second subject in D major, *teneramente, molto cantabile, con espressione* which resembles Don José's D♭ major aria in *Carmen*. This is ostensibly a beautiful love-theme, worked up to a typically ecstatic climax and falling away until a *pp̃ppppp* bassoon solo is left. A *fortissimo* chord suddenly shatters this peace and sets in motion an *Allegro vivo* development section. The death-motto descending motive introduced here is overwhelmingly powerful and awe-inspiring, leading to a version of the orthodox funeral theme 'With the Saints' which almost seems to be mocked at by a shrill renewal of the death-motive. Not even the orgiastic repetition of the second subject in the

[19] EW (2), p. 85.
[20] Eulenburg miniature score, from p. 12 onwards.
[21] ER (2), p. 40.

recapitulation can dispel the underlying terror, which is present even in the soft resigned coda in the tonic major. Here the beautiful phrases for woodwind and horns are underpinned by a measured, funereal *pizzicato* downward scale on the strings – all that is left of the pulsating life of the rest of the movement. Perhaps the most notable feature of all is that there is not a superfluous note in the whole movement. In the terse exposition and succinct development section Tchaikovsky demonstrates that he has learnt how to cut and to prune, and to include only what is essential to the structure.

The lovely five-four 'Valse' which follows gives some respite from the intense drama of the previous movement. That the Schumann-Glinka-Balakirev influence was still at this late stage as much a part of Tchaikovsky's musical make-up as it had ever been is demonstrated by the trio, which starts as shown in Ex. 23.

Compare this with Ex. 16 (p. 105). But in Ex. 23 Tchaikovsky's music is much more threatening. Not only is the downward scale motto used again but the four-square repetition of the material – the four bars quoted are repeated three times without essential change – gives a feeling of throbbing despair, with the continuously repeated crotchet pedal on the bassoons and double basses. Tchaikovsky demonstrates in a masterly fashion that there is still terror lurking in the shadows.

The third movement, *Allegro molto vivace*, starts out as a scherzo of the type used in the Second Symphony, but when that ominous descending scale is introduced,[22] *forte* and *marcato*, accompanied by figures on the brass which resemble the opening four notes of Beethoven's Fifth Symphony (considered in the nineteenth century to be a motive of 'Fate') we know that there is more to the scurrying scherzo figures than would appear on the surface, and that the dotted-note march theme which we have just heard is no military frolic. After a great deal of development the march finally wins the day and the scherzo material is overwhelmed. Tchaikovsky's achievement is to have created a superficially triumphant march in the major mode, in which the underlying feeling of menace becomes more and more apparent; and in the end it is seen that the triumph is for 'Field-Marshal Death' himself.

The climax of the symphony, however, is not in this gigantic march but in the slow finale. The desperate first subject, in the tonic key of B minor, starts with a downward scale heavily disguised for the score

[22] E.M.S., p. 109 *et seq.*

Ex. 23

reader by a curious arrangement of crossing parts, but easy for the listener to distinguish. If this corresponds to the 'Requiem aeternam' then the second subject, which offers some consolation in the relative major, is analogous to the 'Lux perpetua'. But its initial figure is also based on a falling scale, and at the end its appearance in the tonic minor, heralded by a distantly portentous stroke of the gong, is almost unbearably dispairing. In the passionate recapitulation of the first subject the melody is heard without the crossing of parts, so that the strings are individually playing the sinking first subject for the first time. Thus death is no longer hidden, but stares us in the face. The symphony dies away and ends in the darkness from which it had originally emerged.

We know that Gustav Mahler was intimately acquainted with, and greatly admired, *Eugene Onegin*.[23] This admiration, even if it extended to no other music by Tchaikovsky, certainly encompassed the Sixth Symphony as well, since he introduced an *adagio* finale into his Third Symphony, completed in the summer of 1894. Tovey spoke for all

[23] See p. 126 above.

similarly minded persons when he remarked: 'The slow finale [of the Sixth Symphony], with its complete simplicity of despair, is a stroke of genius which solves all the artistic problems that have proved most baffling to symphonic writers since Beethoven.'[24] As far as Mahler is concerned, the *Adagio* finale of his last completed symphony, the Ninth, is much more important than that of his Third Symphony. Its basic mood is one of desolate resignation, and its main theme, like Tchaikovsky's, is based on a downward scale, here derived from the basic 'Lebewohl' ('Farewell') motive of the symphony. The music is not in the least like Tchaikovsky's, but there is a fleeting and possibly subconscious reference to the opening of the Russian folk-song 'Spin, O my spinner', used by Tchaikovsky in his Second Symphony, a few bars after the modulation to C♯ minor.[25] According to Berg, when Mahler was writing his Ninth Symphony he had a premonition of impending death. In this, and in other late works, he has been called the prophet of the age of despair. But if this is so, then he is the Elisha to Tchaikovsky's Elijah.

In Berg's own music the supreme example of a slow finale is to be found in his Lyric Suite for String Quartet (1926), in which the final *Largo desolato* is the psychological climax of a work devoted to increasingly savage contrasts between the frenzied and the forlorn. Another important example of such a finale is the *Lento* from Bartók's Second String Quartet (1917). Like the Berg movement this is not derived in any way from Tchaikovsky's actual music, and unlike Berg's work it is not derived from Mahler either. But the idea of a desolate finale sometimes forlorn, sometimes frenzied, was certainly one which originated in Tchaikovsky's Sixth Symphony. There is another common factor in all these final slow movements: the frequent and crucial changes in tempo. This is an aspect of central European expressionism in which Tchaikovsky's music may safely be said to have had a vital, though not unique, influence.

Another way in which Tchaikovsky influenced Mahler, once again less in the actual music than in the idea – which was however far from being his invention – was in the use of the highly developed symphonic march and symphonic waltz. Tchaikovsky's brilliant adaptation of the intonations of Russian song to the waltz and the march in his last two symphonies is matched by Mahler's equally brilliant adaptation of Austrian song in his later symphonies. Mahler's develop-

[24] EW (2), p. 84.
[25] Bars 31–2. The whole of this movement is derivative, but mostly from Mahler's own music.

ment from the Schubertian military-band type of march theme and fanfare to the tortured horror of the fanfares in the Ninth Symphony, which match the equally doom-laden fanfares to be found in Tchaikovsky's late symphonies, is certainly at least partially a result of the Russian composer's influence. Additionally, the two men had similar temperaments. Both were to some extent social outcasts, Tchaikovsky because of his homosexuality and Mahler because he was a Jew brought up in the Austrian Empire.

Tchaikovsky's music had some influence on three other highly individual composers who have apparently as little in common with each other as with the composers already mentioned: Puccini, Sibelius and Stravinsky. Puccini is perhaps the most obvious of these. The more tortured moments in the relatively early *Tosca* (1900) and the late *Turandot* (1924), for example, have clear antecedents in *The Queen of Spades* and Tchaikovsky's late symphonies. And some of the *tutti* finales of acts in Puccini's operas lean heavily upon Tchaikovsky's methods, with *fortissimo* double-octave doublings of the melody accompanied by feverishly figured sequential skirls, leading to ever more turgescent climaxes. But in certain quieter moments, too, the influence of *Eugene Onegin* is apparent, not only in Puccini's operas but in Massenet's, although here there was a reciprocal influence, and some of Tchaikovsky's more highly scented moments are reminiscent of the French composer.

Hardly less obvious is Tchaikovsky's influence upon the music of Sibelius. Finland was a part of the Russian Empire during Tchaikovsky's lifetime, and both Glinka and Balakirev had made use of Finnish folk-tunes. Robert Layton has remarked upon the 'striking correspondence' between the second group of the first movement of Tchaikovsky's *Souvenir de Florence* and the figure at bar 84 of the slow movement of Sibelius's First Symphony, and he has pointed out that the lush opening theme of this *Andante* and the big tune of the finale 'suggest the higher, more feverish, emotional temperature of the Russian composer'.[26] Other similar examples could be cited, but perhaps of more importance than any such evident derivations is the pre-eminent case of Tchaikovsky's Symphonic Ballad *The Voyevoda*, which was published posthumously in 1897. In this outstanding composition his sometimes interminable sequences have been translated into long *ostinati*, often over pedal points, and the whole lay-out of the score, including much use of the divided strings and some singular

[26] Robert Layton, *Sibelius* (London, 1965), p. 30.

wind-writing, reminds one of Sibelius, as does the depiction of the cold atmosphere of the snowy landscape and the icy finger of death postulated by the story upon which the ballad is based. The themes are equally frigid, quite devoid of the sometimes rather blatant lyricism usually associated with Tchaikovsky. With the exception of certain passages in his previous programme work, *Hamlet*, there is no music of his remotely comparable to this. Had the music been destroyed, as Tchaikovsky wished, we should have been denied a unique glimpse into the way his music might have further developed had he lived.

Oddly enough, though these developments seem to be so radically different from those of Rimsky-Korsakov in his late period, there is one trend that is similar: the greater frigidity of atmosphere. But whereas Tchaikovsky's music was emotionally involved, Rimsky-Korsakov's became emotionally detached, with snatches of folk-like material stripped of their former out-and-out nationalism and recast in the form of an almost transparent mosaic of sound. (Needless to say, the undeviating nationalist Balakirev would have nothing to do with the late works of Tchaikovsky or Rimsky-Korsakov; and as Mussorgsky and Borodin died in the eighteen eighties and Cui turned out to be a musical nonentity, the 'mighty handful' of the sixties and early seventies with which Tchaikovsky had been so closely associated had long since ceased to exist.)

Stravinsky inherited this mathematical emotional detachment from Rimsky-Korsakov, whose pupil he was during the early 1900s. But he was always more willing to acknowledge Tchaikovsky's music than Rimsky-Korsakov's, and it is true that *The Sleeping Beauty* has certain features which both Rimsky-Korsakov and Stravinsky made use of: the puppet-like nature of the characters, so suitable to ballet – perhaps less suitable in Rimsky-Korsakov's operas; the mathematical repetitions required by the dance (and by the choreographer Petipa's precise instructions); and the detached nature of the lyricism necessitated by the fairy-tale world of the ballet. It is not surprising that it was in connection with a revival of *The Sleeping Beauty* by Diaghilev in London that Stravinsky wrote to him the following open letter published in *The Times* of 18 October 1921:

> It gives me great happiness to know that you are producing that masterpiece, *The Sleeping Beauty* by our great and beloved Tchaikovsky ... Tchaikovsky's music, which does not appear specifically Russian to everybody, is often more profoundly Russian than music which has long since been awarded the facile label of Muscovite picturesqueness. This music is quite as Russian as Pushkin's verse or Glinka's song. Whilst not specifically

cultivating in his art the 'soul of the Russian peasant', Tchaikovsky drew unconsciously from the true, popular sources of our race.

And how characteristic were his predilections in the music of the past and of his own day! He worshipped Mozart, Couperin, Glinka, Bizet; that leaves no doubt of the quality of his taste. How strange it is! Every time that a Russian musician has come under the influence of this Latin-Slav culture, and seen clearly the frontier between the Austrian-Catholic Mozart turned towards Beaumarchais, and the German-Protestant Beethoven turned towards Goethe, the result has been striking...

I have just read again the score of this ballet [The Sleeping Beauty]. I have instrumented some numbers of it which had remained unorchestrated and unperformed. I have spent some days of intense pleasure in finding therein again and again the same feeling of freshness, inventiveness, ingenuity and vigour. And I warmly desire that your audiences of all countries may feel this work as it is felt by me, a Russian musician.[27]

A few years later Stravinsky, like Tchaikovsky himself in the *Mozartiana* Suite and Balakirev in the *Chopin* Suite, arranged for orchestra some of Tchaikovsky's lesser-known pieces, making them into the ballet *The Fairy's Kiss*. The difference between Tchaikovsky and Balakirev on the one hand, and Stravinsky on the other, is that the latter has made a 'creative' arrangement and has interpolated newly composed passages at various points in the score which are almost indistinguishable from the original as interpreted by Stravinsky himself. Stravinsky's generous letter and his ballet, however, were not enough to pluck Tchaikovsky's musical reputation from the critical slough into which it had by that time sunk, but from which it has now happily emerged. In his best compositions Tchaikovsky was sometimes able to match his greatest contemporaries, not only in emotional fervour but also in intellectual brilliance. And the popularity of his music has never been greater.

[27] ER (8), pp. 188–9; Eric Walter White, *Stravinsky: The Composer and his Works* (London, 1966), pp. 527–8.

Appendix A

Calendar

(Figures in brackets in last column denote the age at which the person mentioned died; otherwise figures denote the age reached by the person by the end of the year concerned. See Preface for a note on Russian dates.)

Year	Age	Life	Contemporary musicians
1840		Peter Ilyich Tchaikovsky born, 25 April/7 May, at Votkinsk, son of Ilya Petrovich Tchaikovsky, a chief inspector of mines. His brother Nicholas is 2.	Götz born, 7 Dec.; Stainer born, 6 June; Svendsen born, 30 Sept.; Adam aged 37; Alabyev 53; Auber 58; Balakirev 3; Balfe 32; Berlioz 37; Bizet 2; Borodin 6; Brahms 7; Bruch 2; Bruckner 16; Cherubini 80; Chopin 30; Cui 5; Dargomyzhsky 27; Delibes 4; Donizetti 43; Franck 18; Gade 23; Glinka 37; Goldmark 10; Gounod 22; Halévy 41; Heller 26; Henselt 26; Lalo 17; Liszt 29; Lvov 41; Mendelssohn 31; Mercadante 45; Meyerbeer 49; Mussorgsky 1; Offenbach 21; Ponchielli 6; Reinecke 16; Rossini 48; Rubinstein, A. 10; Rubinstein, N. 5; Saint-Saëns 5; Schumann 30; Serov 20; Smetana 16; Spohr 56; Spontini 66; Stassov 16; Strauss (J. ii) 15; Verdi 27; Verstovsky 41; Wagner 27.
1841	1		Chabrier born, 18 Jan.; Dvořák born, 8 Sept.; Pedrell born, 19 Feb.
1842	2	Birth of Tchaikovsky's sister Alexandra (Sasha).	Boïto born, 24 Feb.; Cherubini (82) dies, 15 March; Massenet born, 12 May; Sullivan born, 13 May.
1843	3		Grieg born, 15 June.

Year	Age	Life	Contemporary musicians
1844	4	Starts lessons with Fanny Dürbach, the governess of his elder brother Nicholas and his cousin Lydia. Birth of his brother Hippolyte.	Rimsky-Korsakov born, 6/18 March.
1845	5	Receives piano lessons from Maria Markovna Palchikova and soon becomes more able than his teacher.	Fauré born, 13 May.
1846	6		
1847	7		Mackenzie born, 22 Aug.; Mendelssohn (38) dies, 4 Nov.
1848	8	Removal to Moscow, where his father is disappointed in his prospects of a new appointment, Oct. Fanny Dürbach leaves the family. Removal to St Petersburg, where T. is sent to a boarding school and has music lessons from Filippov.	Donizetti (51) dies, 8 April; Duparc born, 21 Jan.; Parry born, 27 Feb.
1849	9	Severe nervous trouble brought about by overwork at school and abnormal sensitiveness. Removal to Alapayevsk, where T.'s father has secured an appointment at the Yakovlev mines.	Chopin (39) dies, 17 Oct.
1850	10	Sent to School of Jurisprudence in St Petersburg, Aug. Birth of his twin brothers, Anatol and Modest.	
1851	11	Preparatory studies continued at the School of Jurisprudence.	d'Indy born, 27 March; Lortzing (48) dies, 21 Jan.; Spontini (77) dies, 14 Jan.; Alabyev (64) dies, 6 March.
1852	12	Return of the family to St Petersburg.	Stanford born, 30 Sept.
1853	13	Studies at the School of Jurisprudence continued.	
1854	14	Tchaikovsky's mother dies of cholera. Begins to compose.	Humperdinck born, 1 Sept.; Janáček born, 4 July.
1855	15	Has piano lessons with Rudolf Kündinger.	Chausson born, 21 Jan.; Lyadov born, 11 May.
1856	16	Studies at the School of Jurisprudence continued.	Martucci born, 1 Jan.; Schumann (46) dies, 29 July; Sinding born, 11 Jan.; Taneyev born, 13/25 Nov.
1857	17		Elgar born, 2 June; Glinka (54) dies, 3/15 Feb.

Year	Age	Life	Contemporary musicians
1858	18	Studies at the School of Jurisprudence continued.	Leoncavallo born, 2 March; Puccini, born, 22 June; Ethel Smyth born, 23 April.
1859	19	Leaves the School of Jurisprudence and enters the Ministry of Justice as a first-class clerk.	Ippolitov-Ivanov born, 7/19 Nov.; Lyapunov born, 18/30 Nov.; Spohr (75) dies, 22 Oct.
1860	20	Works at the Ministry of Justice, goes to operas, concerts, the theatre, etc.	Albéniz born, 29 May; Charpentier born, 25 June; Mahler born, 7 July; Wolf born, 13 March.
1861	21	Visit to Germany, Belgium, London and Paris with a friend of his father's, July–Sept. Although still holding his post at the Ministry of Justice, he begins to study harmony with Zaremba (40), but is not yet sure that a musician's career is open to him.	Arensky born, 30 July/11 Aug.; Catoire born, 27 April; MacDowell born, 18 Dec.; Marschner (66) dies, 14 Dec.
1862	22	Still continues his studies with Zaremba as an amateur. He enters the newly opened Conservatoire when Zaremba joins the staff there, but still retains his official post.	Debussy born, 22 Aug.; Delius born, 29 Jan.; Halévy (63) dies, 17 March; Verstovsky (63) dies, 5/17 Nov.
1863	23	Resigns his post at the Ministry of Justice, spring. Finds himself in straitened circumstances and ekes out his financial means by giving private lessons. He continues to study theory under Zaremba and goes to A. Rubinstein (33) for composition.	Mascagni born, 7 Dec.
1864	24	Studies at the Conservatoire continued. Overture to Ostrovsky's (41) drama, *The Storm* (Op. 76), composed, summer.	Grechaninov born, 13/25 Oct.; Meyerbeer (73) dies, 2 May; R. Strauss born, 11 June.
1865	25	Conducts the Conservatoire orchestra in his newly composed Overture in F. To A. Rubinstein's annoyance he is absent from the Conservatoire graduating ceremony 31 Dec./12 Jan. N. Rubinstein (30) engages T. as professor of harmony at the recently opened Moscow Conservatoire.	Dukas born, 1 Oct.; Glazunov born, 29 July/10 Aug.; Sibelius born, 8 Dec.
1866	26	Arrival in Moscow, Jan. Composition of First Symphony in	Busoni born, 1 April; Kalinnikov born, 1/13 Jan.;

Year	Age	Life	Contemporary musicians
		G minor (Op. 13) gives him infinite trouble and leads to a nervous breakdown, July. Holiday with his sister's mother-in-law and her daughters Vera and Elizabeth Davydova.	Rebikov born, 20 May/1 June; Satie born, 17 May.
1867	27	Opera *The Voyevoda*, to a libretto partially written by Ostrovsky (44), begun, spring. Visit to Finland. Summer holiday with the Davydova ladies at Hapsal. 3 piano pieces *Souvenir de Hapsal* (Op. 2), dedicated to Vera, who fancies she is in love with him. Return to Moscow, Aug. Meeting with Berlioz, who conducts two concerts there, Dec.	Granados born, 29 July.
1868	28	Visit to St Petersburg where he meets Balakirev (31), Cui (33), Dargomyzhsky (55), Rimsky-Korsakov (24) and Vladimir Stassov (44), spring. Visit to Berlin and Paris with his friend Vladimir Shilovsky and others, summer. *The Voyevoda* put into rehearsal at Moscow. Growing intimacy with Désirée Artôt (33), his engagement to whom he announces to his father, Dec. Symphonic Fantasia *Fatum* finished.	Bantock born, 7 Aug.; Rossini (76) dies, 13 Nov.
1869	29	Artôt marries Mariano Padilla y Ramos (27) but this does not leave Tchaikovsky heartbroken. Production of *The Voyevoda*, 30 Jan./11 Feb. Balakirev performs (and severely criticizes) *Fatum*, 5/17 March. Opera *Undina* composed. After a summer holiday with his sister 'Sasha' Davydova at Kamenka in the Ukraine, he returns to Moscow where he sees Balakirev (32) and meets Borodin (36). Overture-Fantasy *Romeo and Juliet*, suggested by Balakirev, begun. Arrangement for piano duet of	Berlioz (66) dies, 8 March; Dargomyzhsky (56) dies, 5/17 Jan.; Pfitzner born, 5 May; Roussel born, 5 April.

Year	Age	Life	Contemporary musicians
		Fifty Russian Folk-Songs. Composition of Six Songs (Op. 6). Chorus for an opera, *Mandragora*, composed, but the work abandoned, Dec.	
1870	30	Opera *The Oprichnik* begun, Feb. *Romeo and Juliet* performed by N. Rubinstein, 4/16 March. *Undina* rejected by the Theatre Directorate. T. is summoned to Paris to see the consumptive Shilovsky. They go to Soden and attend the Beethoven Centenary Festival at Mannheim. T. visits N. Rubinstein at Wiesbaden. Hasty departure for Switzerland on the outbreak of the Franco-Prussian War, July. After a stay at Interlaken, T. visits Munich and Vienna on his way back to Russia. Return to Moscow, end of Aug. *Romeo and Juliet* revised in accordance with Balakirev's instructions.	Balfe (62) dies, 20 Oct.; Lvov (71) dies, 4/16 Dec.; Mercadante (75) dies, 17 Dec.; Novák born, 5 Dec.; Florent Schmitt born, 28 Sept.
1871	31	First String Quartet in D major (Op. 11) composed and performed, March. Meeting with Turgenyev (53). Summer holidays spent at Kamenka, Nizy and Ussovo with his sister and his friends Kondratyev and Shilovsky respectively.	Auber (89) dies, 12 May; Serov (51) dies, 20 Jan./1 Feb.
1872	32	*The Oprichnik* finished, May. Festival Cantata for the opening of the exhibition celebrating the 200th anniversary of the birth of Peter the Great, 31 May/12 June. Second Symphony in C minor (Op. 17) composed, summer.	Skryabin born, 25 Dec./6 Jan.; Vassilenko born, 18/30 March; Vaughan Williams born, 12 Oct.
1873	33	Second Symphony performed at a Russian Musical Society concert in Moscow, 26 Jan./7 Feb., with great success. Music to Ostrovsky's (50) fairy-tale *Snow Maiden* begun, April. Visit to Germany, Switzerland and Italy, June–Aug. Symphonic Fantasia, based on	Rakhmaninov born, 20 March/1 April; Reger born, 19 March; N. Tcherepnin born, 3/15 May.

146

Year	Age	Life	Contemporary musicians
		Shakespeare's *The Tempest* (Op. 18) with a programme by Stassov, written at Ussovo, Aug. It is first performed in Moscow, Dec.	
1874	34	Second String Quartet in F major (Op. 22) composed, Jan. *The Oprichnik* produced at St Petersburg, 12/24 April. Visit to Italy, spring. Opera *Vakula the Smith*, begun during a holiday at Nizy and finished at Ussovo, end of Aug. Entered for a prize competition a year too early owing to a misunderstanding about dates. First Piano Concerto (Op. 23) composed. Because of N. Rubinstein's (39) strictures it is dedicated to Hans von Bülow, who is effusively grateful.	Holst born, 21 Sept.; Schönberg born, 13 Sept.; Suk born, 4 Jan.
1875	35	Third Symphony in D major (Op. 29) begun at Ussovo, finished Aug. Ballet *Swan Lake* (Op. 20) commissioned by the Moscow Opera. First performance of the First Piano Concerto by von Bülow (45) in Boston, U.S.A. 13/25 October, and of the Third Symphony in Moscow, 7/19 Nov. Taneyev (19) plays the first Moscow performance of the Piano Concerto, 21 Nov./3 Dec. Meeting with Saint-Saëns (40), who visits Moscow, Nov.	Bizet (37) dies, 13 June; Glière born, 11 Jan.; Ravel born, 7 March.
1876	36	T. visits Paris with his brother Modest (25). They go to a performance of Bizet's *Carmen*. Third String Quartet in E♭ minor (Op. 30) begun, Feb. Visit to Vichy for health reasons, July. He goes on to Bayreuth where he meets Liszt (65) and calls on Wagner (63) who fails to receive him. He reports on the first complete performance of the *Ring* for *Russkiye Vedomosti*, Aug. After a visit to his sister at	Falla born, 20 Feb.; Götz (36) dies, 3 Dec.

Year	Age	Life	Contemporary musicians
		Verbovka and Shilovsky at Ussovo he returns to Moscow in great depression. He decides that the best way out of his sexual problems is to marry. Symphonic Fantasia *Francesca da Rimini* (Op. 32) finished, Nov. The opera *Vakula the Smith*, having won the first prize in the competition for which it was entered, produced at St Petersburg, 24 Nov./6 Dec. Meeting with Tolstoy (48) and beginning of correspondence with Nadezhda von Meck (44), who admires T.'s work and is anxious to relieve him of all pecuniary embarrassments, Dec. Variations on a Rococo Theme for cello and orchestra (Op. 33), Dec.	
1877	37	Fourth Symphony in F minor (Op. 36) begun. *Swan Lake* produced in Moscow, 20 Feb/4 March. First performance of *Francesca da Rimini* in Moscow, 25 Feb./9 March. T. again suffers from mental depression, spring. He works at an opera on Pushkin's 'novel in verse' *Eugene Onegin*. Marriage to an infatuated admirer, Antonina Ivanovna Milyukova, 6/18 July. Driven to despair by an irresistible aversion to his wife, he leaves alone for Kamenka, 26 July/7 Aug., where he continues work on the Fourth Symphony and *Eugene Onegin*. Return to his wife in Moscow, Sept. He attempts suicide and then leaves for St Petersburg in a state of mind bordering on madness, 24 Sept./6 Oct., and is ordered a complete change by the doctor. A final separation from his wife is inevitable and he leaves for Switzerland with his brother	Dohnányi born, 27 July.

Year	Age	Life	Contemporary musicians
		Anatol (27), settling at Clarens, Oct. Nadezhda von Meck offers him an annuity of 6,000 roubles. Visits to Italy and Vienna.	
1878	38	Removal to San Remo, Jan., and to Florence, Feb. Fourth Symphony and *Eugene Onegin* finished, Dec./Jan. Return to Clarens, where the Violin Concerto (Op. 35) is composed and the Piano Sonata (Op. 37) is begun, March. The Sonata finished at Verbovka, Aug. Holiday spent at Brailov, the estate of Nadezhda von Meck (46), who is absent, May. Return to Moscow, Sept. He finds his duties at the Conservatoire quite unbearable and resigns his professorship. Begins First Orchestral Suite (Op. 43) at Kamenka. Departure for Florence, Nov. Begins opera *The Maid of Orleans*.	
1879	39	Visits Clarens and Paris. Returns to Russia for a student production of *Eugene Onegin* in Moscow, 17/29 March. Summer again spent at Kamenka and Brailov. When Nadezhda von Meck (47) returns home, Aug., T. moves on to her smaller house at Simaki nearby. They meet one day by mistake but do not speak to one another. Their friendship is epistolary only. Second Piano Concerto in G major (Op. 44) begun at Kamenka, Oct. Departure for the West, Nov.	Frank Bridge born, 26 Feb.; Ireland born, 13 Aug.; Respighi born, 9 July; Cyril Scott born, 27 Sept.
1880	40	Italian Capriccio for orchestra (Op. 45) begun in Rome. Death of father, 9/21 Jan. Return to Russia, March. The Capriccio finished at Kamenka, spring. Visits Brailov and Simaki, summer. Serenade for Strings (Op. 48) and *1812* Overture	Bloch born, 24 July; Medtner born, 24 Dec./5 Jan.; Offenbach (61) dies, 4 Oct.; Pizzetti born, 20 Sept.; Wieniawski (45) dies, 31 March.

Year	Age	Life	Contemporary musicians
		(Op. 49) finished at Kamenka, Oct. The latter was commissioned by N. Rubinstein for the Moscow Exhibition.	
1881	41	Production of *The Maid of Orleans* at the Maryinsky Theatre, St Petersburg, 13/25 Feb. After a visit to Italy and France the Directorship of the Moscow Conservatoire, vacated by the death of N. Rubinstein, is offered to T., who declines it, April. Balakirev (44) also declines it, but Hubert (41) accepts. T. spends the summer at Kamenka editing the Russian church music of Bortnyansky, which he 'loathes'. Visits Rome and again meets Liszt (70). First performance of the Violin Concerto by Adolf Brodsky in Vienna, 22 Nov./4 Dec. Hanslick (56) criticizes it vituperatively.	Bartók born, 25 March; Myaskovsky born, 8/20 April; Mussorgsky (42) dies, 16/28 March; N. Rubinstein (46) dies, 11/23 March; Vieuxtemps (61) dies, 6 June.
1882	42	First performance of Serenade for Strings in Moscow, 16/28 Jan. Piano Trio (Op. 50) dedicated to the memory of N. Rubinstein, finished, Jan. First performance, at the Moscow Art and Industrial Exhibition, of the Second Piano Concerto, with Taneyev (26) as soloist, 18/30 May, and the *1812* Overture, 8/20 Aug., at the consecration of the Cathedral of the Redeemer in the Kremlin.	Kodály born, 16 Dec.; Malipiero born, 18 March; Raff (60) dies; Stravinsky born, 5/17 June.
1883	43	Visits to Berlin and Paris, Jan.–May. Opera *Mazeppa*, based on Pushkin's poem, *Poltava*, finished, spring. Second Orchestral Suite (Op. 53) finished at Kamenka.	Bax born, 6 Nov.; Casella born, 25 July; Flotow (71) dies, 24 Jan.; Gnyessin born, 23 Jan./4 Feb.; A. Krein born, 8/20 Oct.; Szymanowski born, 21 Sept.; Varèse born, 22 Dec.; Wagner (69) dies, 13 Feb.; Webern born, 3 Dec.
1884	44	Productions of *Mazeppa* in Moscow and St Petersburg, Feb. Third Orchestral Suite (Op. 55) finished, July. Command performance of *Eugene Onegin*	Smetana (60) dies, 12 May.

Year	Age	Life	Contemporary musicians
		at the Imperial Opera in St Petersburg.	
1885	45	Rents a house at Maidanovo near Klin, Feb. Is elected a director of the Moscow branch of the Russian Musical Society. Composition of the *Manfred* Symphony, undertaken on Balakirev's (48) advice, finished and that of the opera *The Sorceress* begun, Sept.	Berg born, 7 Feb.; Wellesz born, 21 Oct.
1886	46	First performance of *Manfred* in Moscow, March. Visit to Tiflis, where the Musical Society gives a concert and dinner in his honour, April. May and June spent in Paris, where he meets Delibes (50), Fauré (41), Lalo (63), Thomas (75) and Pauline Viardot-Garcia (65). Return to Maidanovo, end of June.	Liszt (75) dies, 31 July; Ponchielli (52) dies, 17 Jan.
1887	47	First performance of *Cherevichki*, a new version of *Vakula the Smith*, 19/31 Jan., conducted by T. himself, who also makes an appearance as concert conductor, at St Petersburg, with a programme of his own works, 5/17 March. Visit to his brother Anatol at Tiflis. Composes *Mozartiana* Suite (Op. 61). Goes to Aachen to see his friend Kondratyev who is critically ill. Unsuccessful production of *The Sorceress* at St Petersburg, 20 Oct./1 Nov., but T.'s conducting of it praised.	Borodin (54) dies, 16/28 Feb.
1888	48	Begins his first international tour as conductor at Leipzig, where he meets Brahms (55), Grieg (44) and Ethel Smyth (30). He conducts the Gewandhaus orchestra, Jan. Concerts conducted at Hamburg and Berlin, where he sees Désirée Artôt (53) again. Visit to Prague, where he gives two concerts and meets Dvořák	Alexandrov born, 13/25 May; Alkan (75) dies, 29 March.

Year	Age	Life	Contemporary musicians
		(47), Feb. Arrival in Paris, 12/24 Feb. Two concerts given there. Meeting with Gounod, Massenet and others. Conducts one R.P.S. concert in London, March. After his return to Russia, T. takes possession of a house at Frolovskoye, April. Fifth Symphony in E minor (Op. 64) finished, Aug. First performances, in St Petersburg, of the Fifth Symphony, 5/17 Nov., and of the Overture-Fantasy *Hamlet* (Op. 67), 12/24 Nov. Visit to Prague to conduct *Eugene Onegin*, Nov.	
1889	49	Second international concert tour. T. conducts at Cologne, Frankfurt, Dresden, Geneva and Hamburg, Feb./March. Visit to Paris and conducts another R.P.S. concert in London, April. Ballet, *The Sleeping Beauty* (Op. 66) finished at Frolovskoye, summer. T. conducts festival in honour of Rubinstein, (59) for which he has composed *Greeting to A. G. Rubinstein* and an Impromptu for piano, Nov.	Henselt (75) dies, 28 Sept./10 Oct.
1890	50	Production of *The Sleeping Beauty* in St Petersburg, 3/15 Jan. Opera, *The Queen of Spades*, to a libretto of his brother Modest (40), based on Pushkin, composed in Florence, Jan.–March. String Sextet, *Souvenir de Florence* (Op. 70) composed at Frolovskoye, June. Rupture with Nadezhda von Meck (58), Sept. Composition of the Symphonic Ballad, *The Voyevoda* (Op. 78). *The Queen of Spades* produced in St Petersburg with triumphant success, 7/19 Dec.	Franck (68) dies, 8 Nov.; Gade (73) dies, 21 Dec.; Ibert born, 15 Aug.; Frank Martin born, 15 Sept.; Martinů born, 8 Dec.
1891	51	Performance of Shakespeare's *Hamlet* with incidental music (Op. 67a) by T., 9/21 Feb. St Petersburg Opera commissions	Bliss born, 2 Aug.; Delibes (55) dies, 16 Jan.; Prokofiev born, 11/23 April.

Year	Age	Life	Contemporary musicians
		a one-act opera, *Iolanta*, and a ballet, *Nutcracker*, Feb. Visit to Paris in a state of nervous depression, March, en route for the U.S.A. Hears of the death of his sister 'Sasha' (48). Arrival in New York, 14/26 April. Concerts conducted in New York, Baltimore and Philadelphia. First performance of the Symphonic Ballad *The Voyevoda*, at Siloti's (28) concert in Moscow, 6/18 Nov.	
1892	52	Performance of *Eugene Onegin* conducted by Mahler (32) at Hamburg in the presence of T., who is very impressed. First performance of the *Nutcracker* Suite in St Petersburg, 7/19 March. After a visit to Vichy with his nephew Vladimir ('Bob') Davydov (21), T. sets to work on a Symphony in E flat at his new country house at Klin, summer. Visits to Vienna, Salzburg and Prague. Production of *Iolanta* and the *Nutcracker* ballet in St Petersburg, 6/18 December. Visits Fanny Dürbach in Switzerland.	Honegger born, 10 March; Lalo (69) dies, 22 April; Milhaud born, 4 Sept.
1893	53	Concert conducted at Brussels, 2/14 Jan. After some performances conducted at Odessa, T. returns to Klin, Feb. He abandons last year's sketches for a symphony and sets to work on the Sixth Symphony in B minor (Op. 74) (*Pathétique*), sketches a Concerto movement derived from the discarded symphony, writes 18 piano pieces (Op. 72) and Six Songs (Op. 73). Royal Philharmonic concert conducted in London 20 May/1 June. At Cambridge the honorary degree of Doctor of Music is conferred on T., Boito (51), Bruch (55), Saint-Saëns (58) and Grieg (50), the last being	Gounod (75) dies, 18 Oct.; Albéniz 33; Alexandrov 5; Arensky 32; Balakirev 56; Bantock 25; Bartók 12; Bax 10; Berg 8; Bliss 2; Bloch 13; Boïto 51; Brahms 60; Bridge 14; Bruch 55; Bruckner 69; Busoni 27; Casella 10; .Catoire 32; Chabrier 52; Chausson 38; Cui 58; Debussy 31; Delius 31; Dohnányi 16; Dukas 28; Duparc 45; Dvořák 52; Elgar 36; Falla 17; Fauré 48; Glazunov 28; Glière 17; Gnyessin 10; Goldmark 63; Granados 26; Grechaninov 29; Grieg 50; Holst 19; Honegger 1; Humperdinck 39; d'Indy 42; Ippolitov-Ivanov 34; Ireland 14; Janáček 39; Kalinnikov 27; Kodály 11; Koreschenko 23;

Tchaikovsky

Year	Age	Life	Contemporary musicians

absent, 1/13 June. A concert of works by these composers and by Stanford (41) is given. Return to Russia, 18/30 June. Sixth Symphony performed in St Petersburg under T.'s direction, 16/28 Oct. He dies there on 25 Oct/6 Nov. The manner of his death has been a cause of controversy: either, as alleged by Alexandra Orlova, he committed suicide by taking poison, after a 'kangaroo' court of his contemporaries at the School of Jurisprudence had insisted on this to avoid a scandal over a homosexual episode which would have brought disrepute to the school, or, as stated by Modest in his biography of T., he died of cholera.

G. Krein 13; A. Krein 10; Leoncavallo 35; Lyadov 38; Lyapunov 34; MacDowell 32; Mackenzie 46; Mahler 33; Malipiero 11; Massenet 51; Mascagni 30; Medtner 13; Myaskovsky 12; Milhaud 1; Novák 23; Parry 45; Pedrell 52; Pfitzner 24; Pizzetti 13; Prokofiev 2; Puccini 35; Rakhmaninov 20; Ravel 18; Rebikov 27; Reger 20; Reinecke 69; Respighi 14; Rimsky-Korsakov 49; Roussel 24; A. Rubinstein 63; Saint-Saëns 58; Schmitt 23; Schoenberg 19; Scott 14; Skryabin 21; Sibelius 28; Sinding 36; Smyth 35; Sokolov 34; Stainer 53; Stanford 41; Stassov 69; Strauss (J. ii) 68; R. Strauss 29; Stravinsky 11; Suk 19; Sullivan 51; Svendsen 53; Szymanowski 10; Taneyev 37; N. Tcherepnin 20; Thomas 82; Vassilenko 21; Vaughan Williams 21; Wolf 33.

Appendix B

List of works

Dramatic works

(a) OPERAS

Opus no.

3   *The Voyevoda* (libretto by A. N. Ostrovsky and Tchaikovsky, based on Ostrovsky), 1867–8.

—   *Undina* (libretto by Vernoy de Saint-Georges, translated by F. A. Sollogub, based on La Motte Fouqué's *Ondine*), 1869. (Both these early operas were plundered later, and the music not made use of elsewhere was largely destroyed.)

—   *The Oprichnik* (libretto by Tchaikovsky after Lazhechnikov), 1870–2. First wholly extant opera.

14   *Vakula the Smith* (libretto by Polonsky after Gogol), 1874. Revised as *Cherevichki*, 1885.

24   *Eugene Onegin* (libretto by Tchaikovsky with the initial participation of K. S. Shilovsky, after Pushkin), 1877–8. Écossaise for sixth scene added 1885.

—   *The Maid of Orleans* (libretto by Tchaikovsky, based on Zhukovsky's translation of Schiller's *Jungfrau von Orleans*), 1878–9. Some alterations made, 1882.

—   *Mazeppa* (libretto by V. P. Burenin and Tchaikovsky, after Pushkin's *Poltava*), 1881–3.

—   *The Sorceress* (libretto by I. V. Shpazhinsky), 1885–7.

68   *The Queen of Spades* (libretto by M. I. Tchaikovsky with some assistance from Tchaikovsky, after Pushkin), 1890.

69   *Iolanta* (libretto by Hetrz/Zotov/M. I. Tchaikovsky), 1891.

(b) BALLETS

20   *Swan Lake*, 1875–6.

66   *The Sleeping Beauty*, 1888–9.

71   *Nutcracker*, 1891–2.

(c) INCIDENTAL MUSIC, OTHER STAGE MUSIC, FRAGMENTS, ETC.

—   *Boris Godunov* (Pushkin). Music for the Fountain Scene, ?1863–4; not extant.

—   *The Muddle* (P. S. Federov). Couplets for this vaudeville, 1867; not extant.

—   Introduction to Act I and Mazurka for Ostrovsky's *Dmitry the Pretender and Vassily Shuisky*, before 30 Jan. 1867.

155

Tchaikovsky

Opus no.

—   Recitatives and choruses for Auber's *Le Domino Noir*, 1868; not extant.
—   Chorus of Flowers and Insects for projected opera *Mandragora*, 1869.
—   Couplets 'Vous l'ordonnez' from Beaumarchais' *Le Barbier de Séville*, 1872.
12   Incidental Music to Ostrovsky's *Snow Maiden*, 1873.
—   Recitatives for Mozart's *The Marriage of Figaro*, 1875.
—   Lullaby for Octave Feuillet's play *La Fée*, 1879.
—   Melodrama for small orchestra, for the Domovoy scene in Ostrovsky's *The Voyevoda*, 1886.
67a   Incidental music to *Hamlet*, 1891.
—   Duet from *Romeo and Juliet* (partly based on Overture-Fantasy. Sketch for an opera?); completed by Taneyev, 1893.

Orchestral Works

—   Andante ma non troppo in A major, for small orchestra, 1863–4.
—   Agitato in E minor, for small orchestra, 1863–4.
—   Introduction and little Allegro in D major, for small orchestra, 1863–4.
—   Allegro vivo in C minor for small orchestra, 1863–4.
—   *The Romans in the Coliseum*, 1863–4? not extant.
76   Overture to Ostrovsky's *The Storm*, 1864.
—   Characteristic Dances (1865); revised and used in the opera *The Voyevoda*, 1868.
—   Overture in F major for small orchestra, 1865; rescored for full symphony orchestra, 1866.
—   Concert Overture in C minor, 1866.
13   Symphony No. 1 in G minor (*Winter Reveries*), 1866, rev. 1874.
15   Festival Overture on the Danish National Anthem, 1866.
77   Symphonic Fantasia *Fatum*, 1868.
—   Overture *Romeo and Juliet*, 1869; rev. 1870 and further rev. and restyled 'Overture-Fantasy', 1880.
17   Symphony No. 2 in C minor, 1872, rev. 1879.
—   Serenade for Small Orchestra, for Nicholas Rubinstein's name-day, 1872.
18   *The Tempest* (symphonic *Fantasia* based on Shakespeare's play), 1873.
29   Symphony No. 3 in D major, 1875.
31   Slavonic March (originally styled Serbo-Russian March), 1876.
32   *Francesca da Rimini* (symphonic *Fantasia* after Dante), 1876.
36   Symphony No. 4 in F minor, 1877–8.
43   Suite No. 1 in D major, 1878–9.
45   Italian Capriccio, 1880.
—   Musical Picture, *Montenegrin Villagers receiving news of Russia's declaration of war on Turkey*, 1880; not extant.
49   *The Year 1812*, Festival Overture, 1880.
—   Coronation March, 1883.
53   Suite No. 2 in C major, 1883.
55   Suite No. 3 in G major, 1884.

Opus no.

58	Symphony, *Manfred* (after Byron), 1885.
—	Jurists' March, 1885.
64	Symphony No. 5 in E minor, 1888.
67	Overture-Fantasy, *Hamlet*, 1888.
78	Symphonic Ballad, *The Voyevoda* (nothing to do with the opera of the same name), 1890–1.
71a	*Nutcracker* Suite, 1892.
74	Symphony No. 6 in B minor (*Pathétique*), 1893.

Works for Solo Instrument and Orchestra

23	Piano Concerto No. 1 in B♭ minor, 1874–5.
26	*Sérénade Mélancolique*, for violin and orchestra, 1875.
33	Variations on a Rococo Theme, for cello and orchestra, 1876.
34	Valse-Scherzo, for violin and orchestra, 1877.
35	Violin Concerto in D major, 1878.
44	Piano Concerto No. 2 in G major, 1879–80; rev. by A. I. Siloti with the approval of the composer, 1893.
56	Concert Fantasia, for piano and orchestra, 1884.
62	*Pezzo capriccioso*, for cello and orchestra, 1887.
75	Piano Concerto No. 3 in E♭ major (in one movement), 1893.
79	Andante and Finale for piano and orchestra, 1893, orchestrated by Taneyev. (Ops. 75 and 79 originated as movements of a Symphony in E♭ major, which has recently been reconstructed.)

Works for String Orchestra

48	Serenade in C major, 1880.
—	Elegy in honour of I. V. Samarin, 1884. (Used in the Incidental Music to *Hamlet*, 1891.)

Chamber Music

The following are all student works dating from 1863–4, without opus number:

Adagio in F major, for wind octet.
Introduction and allegro in A major, for two flutes, string quartet and double bass.
Allegro in C minor, for string quartet, double bass and piano.
Adagio molto in E♭ major, for string quartet and harp.
Allegro ma non tanto in G major, for string quartet and double bass.
Prelude in E minor, for string quartet and double bass.
Fragment of Andante molto in G major, for string quartet.
Allegro vivace in B♭ major, for string quartet.
Allegretto in E major, for string quartet.
Adagio in C major, for four horns.
Allegretto in D major, for violin, viola and cello.

Some of these exercises may have been orchestral sketches.

Tchaikovsky

Opus no.

—   String Quartet in B♭ major (only the first Allegro is extant), 1865.

11   String Quartet No. 1 in D major, 1871. The Andante cantabile was scored for cello and orchestra in the late eighties, and this slow movement was performed by string orchestra with Tchaikovsky's approval during his lifetime.

22   String Quartet No. 2 in F major, 1874.

30   String Quartet No. 3 in E♭ minor, 1876.

42   *Souvenir d'un lieu cher* for violin and piano, 1878.

50   Trio for piano, violin and cello, 1881–2.

70   String Sextet (*Souvenir de Florence*), 1890–2.

Piano Music

—   *Valse dédié à Mlle. Anastasie*, 1854.

—   Piece (on a theme 'By the River, by the Bridge'), 1862; not extant.

—   Fragment of an Allegro in F minor, 1863–4.

—   Theme and Variations in A minor, 1863–4.

80   Sonata in C♯ minor, 1865.

1   *Scherzo à la Russe*; Impromptu in E♭ minor, 1867.

2   *Souvenir de Hapsal* Nos. 1 and 3, 1867; No. 2, 1863–5?

—   Potpourri on Motives from P. Tchaikovsky's opera *The Voyevoda* (published under the pseudonym H. Cramer), 1868.

4   Valse-Caprice in D major, 1868.

5   Romance in F minor, 1868.

7   Valse-Scherzo in A major, 1870.

8   *Capriccio* in G♭ major, 1870.

9   Rêverie, Salon Polka, Salon Mazurka, 1870.

10   Nocturne and Humoresque, 1871; the Humoresque arr. for violin and piano *c.* 1877.

19   Six Pieces, 1873. No. 4, Nocturne, arr. for cello and orchestra in the late eighties.

21   Six Pieces on one theme, 1873.

37b Twelve pieces, *The Seasons*, 1876.

—   Funeral March for piano duet (on themes from *The Oprichnik*), 1877; not extant.

—   The Russian Volunteer Fleet (sometimes referred to as 'Skobelev March'; published under the pseudonym P. Sinopov), 1878.

37   Sonata in G major, 1878.

39   Children's Album (twenty-four easy pieces), 1878.

40   Twelve pieces of moderate difficulty, 1878; first version of No. 9, 1876.

51   Six Pieces, 1882.

—   Impromptu-Capriccio, 1885.

59   Dumka, 1886.

—   Valse-Scherzo No. 2, 1889.

—   Impromptu in A♭ major, 1889.

—   Military March for the 98th Yurevsky Infantry Regiment, 1893. (Not intended as a piano piece but as the short score of a piece for military band.)

Opus no.

72 Eighteen Pieces, 1893.
— 'Aveu passioni' in E minor, 1892?
— *Momento lirico*, completed by Taneyev.

Vocal Music[1]

(a) SONGS
— 'My genius, my angel, my friend' (Fet), 1857–60.
— 'Song of Zemfira' (Pushkin), 1857–60.
— 'Who goes...' (Apukhtin), 1857–60.
— 'Mezza Notte' (In Italian; author unknown), 1857–60.
6 Six Songs, 1869: 1. 'Do not believe, my friend' (A. K. Tolstoy); 2. 'Not a word, O my friend' (Hartmann/Pleshcheyev); 3. 'Painfully and sweetly' (E. P. Rostopchina); 4. 'A tear trembles' (A. K. Tolstoy); 5. Russian translation by Mey of Heine's 'Warum sind dann die Rosen so blass?' ('Why?'); 6. Mey's translation of Goethe's 'Nur wer die Sehnsucht kennt', usually known in this country as 'None but the Lonely Heart'.
— 'To forget so soon' (Apukhtin), 1870.
16 Six Songs, 1872: 1. 'Lullaby' (Maikov); 2. 'Wait' (Grekov); 3. 'Accept just once' (Fet); 4. 'O sing that song' (Hemans/Pleshcheyev); 5. 'Thy radiant image' (Tchaikovsky); 6. 'New Greek Song' (Maikov). Tchaikovsky arr. Nos. 1, 4 and 5 for piano, and No. 4 for violin and piano.
— 'Take my heart away' (Fet), 1873.
— 'Blue eyes of spring' (Heine/Mikhailov), 1873.
25 Six Songs, 1874: 1. 'Reconciliation' (Shcherbina); 2. 'As o'er the burning ashes' (Tyutchev); 3. 'Mignon's Song' (Goethe/Tyutchev); 4. 'The Canary' (Mey); 5. 'I never spoke to her' (Mey); 6. 'As they kept on saying, "fool"' (Mey).
— 'I should like in a single word' (Heine/Mey), 1875.
— 'We have not far to walk' (Grekov), 1875.
27 Six Songs, 1875: 1. 'To sleep' (Ogarev); 2. 'Look, yonder cloud' (Grekov); 3. 'Do not leave me' (Fet); 4. 'Evening' (Schevchenko/Mey); 5. 'Was it the mother who bore me' (Mickiewicz/Mey); 6. 'My spoiled darling' (Mickiewicz/Mey).
28 Six Songs, 1875: 1. 'No, I shall never tell' (de Musset/Grekov); 2. 'The Corals' (Syrokomla/Mey); 3. 'Why did I dream of you?' (Mey); 4. 'He loved me so much' (Apukhtin); 5. 'No response or word of greeting' (Apukhtin); 6. 'The fearful minute' (Tchaikovsky).
— 'The underdog' (musical joke) (Tchaikovsky), 1876.
38 Six Songs, 1878: 1. 'Don Juan's Serenade' (A. K. Tolstoy); 2. 'It was in the early spring' (A. K. Tolstoy); 3. 'Mid the din of the ball' (A. K. Tolstoy); 4. 'If thou couldst for one moment' (A. K. Tolstoy); 5. 'Love of a corpse' (Lermontov); 6. 'Pimpinella' (Tchaikovsky from an Italian popular song).

[1]In order to avoid adding to the already confusingly large numbers of translations of the song titles, Gerald Abraham's translations are used here.

Opus no.

47   Seven Songs, 1880: 1. 'If only I'd known' (A. K. Tolstoy); 2. 'Softly the spirit flew up to heaven' (A. K. Tolstoy); 3. 'Dusk fell on the earth' (Mickiewicz/N. V. Berg); 4. 'Sleep, my poor friend' (A. K. Tolstoy); 5. 'I bless you, forests' (A. K. Tolstoy), sometimes known as 'Benediction'; 6. 'Does the day reign' (Apukhtin), accomp. orch. by T., 1888; 7. 'Was I not a little blade of grass in the field' (Shevchenko/Surikov), accomp. orch. by T., 1884.

54   Sixteen Songs for Children (No. 16, 1881; Nos. 1–15, 1883) (Nos. 1–14, Pleshcheyev; No. 15, Lenartowicz/Surikov; No. 16, Aksakov): 1. 'Granny and Grandson'; 2. 'Little Bird' (from the Polish); 3. 'Spring' (from the Polish); 4. 'My little garden'; 5. 'A legend: The Christ-child had a garden' (from the English), accomp. orch. by T., 1884, arr. for mixed chorus *a cappella*, 1889; 6. 'On the bank'; 7. 'Winter evening'; 8. 'The cuckoo' (from the German); 9. 'The snow's already melting' ('Spring'); 10. 'Lullaby in a storm'; 11. 'The flower' (after L. Ratisbon); 12. 'Winter'; 13. 'Spring song'; 14. 'Autumn'; 15. 'The swallow'; 16. 'Child's song'.

57   Six Songs, 1884: 1. 'Tell me, what in the shade of the branches' (Sollogub); 2. 'On the golden cornfields' (A. K. Tolstoy); 3. 'Heiss mich nicht reden' (Goethe) in a Russian translation by Strugovshchikov; 4. 'Sleep!' (Merezhkovsky); 5. 'Death' (Merezhkovsky); 6. 'Only thou' (Kristen/Pleshcheyev).

60   Twelve Songs, 1886: 1. 'Last night' (Khomyakov); 2. 'I'll tell thee nothing' (Fet); 3. 'O, if you knew' (Pleshcheyev); 4. 'The nightingale' (Stefanovic/Pushkin); 5. 'Simple words' (Tchaikovsky); 6. 'Frenzied nights' (Apukhtin); 7. 'Song of the Gypsy girl' (Polonsky); 8. 'Forgive!' (Nekrasov); 9. 'Night' (Polonsky); 10. 'Behind the window, in the shadow' (Polonsky); 11. 'Exploit' (Khomyakov); 12. 'The mild stars shone for us' (Polonsky).

63   Six Songs, 1887 (Grand Duke Constantine): 1. 'I did not love thee at first'; 2. 'I opened the window'; 3. 'I do not please you'; 4. 'The first tryst'; 5. 'The fires in the rooms were already extinguished'; 6. 'Serenade'.

65   Six French Songs, 1888 (Nos. 2, 3, 4 and 6, Paul Collin, No. 1, E. Turquety, No. 5, A. M. Blanchecotte): 1. 'Aurore'; 2. 'Déception'; 3. 'Sérénade'; 4. 'Poème d'octobre'; 5. 'Les larmes'; 6. 'Rondel'.

—   Musical Jest (plea to the composer's nephew, V. L. Davydov), 1892.

73   Six Songs, 1893 (D. M. Rathaus): 1. 'We sat together'; 2. 'Night'; 3. 'In this moonlight'; 4. 'The sun has set'; 5. 'Mid sombre days'; 6. 'Again, as before, alone'.

(b) VOCAL DUETS

46   Six Duets, 1880: 1. 'Evening' (Surikov); 2. 'Scottish Ballad: Edward' (trans. A. K. Tolstoy); 3. 'Tears' (Tyutchev); 4. 'In the garden near the ford' (Shevchenko/Surikov); 5. 'Passion spent' (A. K. Tolstoy); 6. 'Dawn' (Surikov), later orch. by T.

Opus no.

(c) CHORAL WORKS

— Unnamed oratorio, 1863–4; not extant.

— A *cappella* chorus, 'To sleep' (Ogarev) 1863–4; revised and orch. accomp. added *c.* 1864.

— 'An die Freude', cantata for four soloists, chorus and orchestra (Schiller/Aksakov), 1865.

— 'Nature and love' (Tchaikovsky) for two sopranos, contralto and piano, 1870.

— Cantata for tenor solo, chorus and orchestra, for the Opening of the Polytechnic Exhibition in Moscow (Polonsky), 1872.

— Cantata for tenor solo, chorus and orchestra, for the jubilee of O. A. Petrov, 1875.

41   Liturgy of St John Chrysostom (four-part mixed chorus; 15 numbers), 1878.

52   Vesper Service (harmonization of 17 liturgical chants for mixed chorus), 1881–2.

— 'Evening' (anon.), three-part male chorus *a cappella*, 1881.

— Cantata for the pupils of the Patriotic Institute (four-part female chorus *a cappella*), 1881 (not extant).

— Coronation Cantata 'Moscow' for mezzo-soprano and baritone soli, chorus and orchestra (Maikov), 1883.

— Three Cherubic Hymns (mixed voices *a cappella*), 1884.

— Hymn to St Cyril and St Methodius for *a cappella* chorus (based on a Czech melody; Russian words by Tchaikovsky), 1885.

— Six Church Songs (Anthems) for *a cappella* four-part chorus, 1885.

— Chorus *a cappella*, for the Fiftieth Anniversary of the Imperial School of Jurisprudence (Tchaikovsky), 1885.

— 'The golden cloud had slept' (Lermontov) for mixed voices *a cappella*, 1887.

— Male chorus *a cappella*, dedicated to the students of Moscow University (Grand Duke Constantine), 1887.

— 'The nightingale' (Tchaikovsky), *a cappella* chorus, 1889.

— Greeting to A. G. Rubinstein, *a cappella* chorus (Polonsky), 1889.

— 'Tis not the cuckoo in the damp pinewood', *a cappella* chorus (Tsyganov), 1891.

— 'The merry voice grew silent', male chorus *a cappella* (Pushkin), 1891.

— 'Without time or season', female chorus *a cappella* (Tsyganov), 1891.

— 'An angel crying', chorus *a cappella* (date unknown).

— 'Spring', female chorus *a cappella* (date unknown) (not extant).

Arrangements of the Works of Other Composers

(a) ORCHESTRATIONS

— *Beethoven:* Piano Sonata, Op. 31, No. 2, first movt., 1863.

— *Beethoven: Kreutzer* Sonata, first movt., 1863–4.

— *Gung'l:* Valse, 1863–4.

— *Schumann: Études Symphoniques, Adagio* and *Allegro brillante*, 1863–4.

— *Weber:* Piano Sonata in A♭ major, Op. 39, scherzo, 1863–4.

Tchaikovsky

Opus no.

—   *Kral, K. I.:* Triumphal March, 1867.
—   *Dubuque:* Polka, *Mariya-Dagmar*, 1869.
—   *Stradella:* Aria, 'O del mio dolce', 1870.
—   *Cimarosa:* Trio from *Il matrimonio segreto*, 1870?
—   *Dargomyzhsky:* Trio, 'The golden cloud had slept', 1870?
—   *Haydn:* Austrian National Anthem, 1874.
—   *Liszt: König von Thule*, 1874.
—   *Schumann:* Ballade vom Haideknaben, 1874.
61   *Mozart:* Suite No. 4, *Mozartiana* (Gigue, K.574; Minuet, K.355; Liszt's transcription of 'Ave verum corpus', K.618); Variations on a theme by Gluck, K.455 (with minor alterations), 1887.
—   *Laroche:* Fantasy-overture, 1888.
—   *Menter, Sophie: Ungarische Zigeunerweisen*, 1893.

(b) PIANO ARRANGEMENTS
—   *Dargomyzhsky: Kazachok* (solo), 1868.
—   *Dubuque: Romance de Tarnowsky* (duet), 1868.
—   *Meyerbeer:* Potpourri on *Pardon de Ploërmel* under the pseudonym H. Cramer (duet), 1868–9.
—   *Anon.:* Fifty Russian Folk-songs (duet), 1868–9.
—   *Rubinstein, A.:* Musical Picture *Ivan the Terrible* (duet), 1869.
—   *Rubinstein, A.:* Musical Picture *Don Quixote* (duet), 1870.
—   *Mamontova, M.:* Piano accompaniments to *Children's Songs*, based on Russian and Ukrainian melodies, 1872 and 1877.
—   *Weber:* Piano Sonata, Op. 39, perpetuum mobile (for left hand only).

(c) CHORAL ARRANGEMENTS
—   *Anon.:* 'Gaudeamus igitur' (male chorus and piano).
—   *Glinka: Slavsya* from *A Life for the Tsar* simplified and linked with the Imperial Russian National Anthem (Massed chorus and orchestra), 1883.
—   *Mozart:* 'Night' (Tchaikovsky). Vocal quartet (S.A.T.B.) based on Fantasia in C minor, K.475, *andantino*, 1893.

Editorial Works

Prokunin, V.: Sixty-six Russian Folk-songs, 1872.
Bortnyansky, D.: Complete edition of the Church Music, in 12 volumes, 1881.

Literary Works

'Guide to the Practical Study of Harmony', 1871.
'Short Manual of Harmony, adapted to the Study of Religious Music in Russia', 1874. Text for a vocal quartet by Glinka, 1877.
Numerous Musical Criticisms; Diaries (see Appendix D for these); parts of libretti for his own operas, verses for songs and cantatas (see above); translations of the text of songs by A. Rubinstein and Glinka; translation of the libretto of *The Marriage of Figaro* and of the Page's cavatina from Meyerbeer's *Les*

Opus no.

Huguenots; translations of Gevaert's 'Traité d'Instrumentation', Schumann's 'Musikalische Haus- und Lebensregeln', J. C. Lobe's 'Katechismus der Musik'.

Appendix C

Personalia

Albrecht, Karl, a native of Breslau, for twelve years conductor at the Imperial opera in St Petersburg. His son Constantine (1836–93) was a cellist and choirmaster who became inspector of the Moscow Conservatoire and Nicholas Rubinstein's 'right hand'. He married in 1862 the daughter of an eminent professor of the piano, Langer.

Artôt, Marguerite Joséphine Désirée Montagney (1835–1907), Belgian operatic mezzo-soprano singer, daughter of a professor of the horn at the Brussels Conservatoire, but born in Paris. Pupil of Pauline Viardot-Garcia (q.v.). First sang at concerts in Belgium, Holland and England, but joined the Paris Opéra in 1858. Later appeared in Italy, Germany and Russia. Married Padilla (q.v.) in 1869.

Auber, Daniel François Esprit (1782–1871), French composer, mainly of operas, including *La Muette de Portici, Fra Diavolo* and *Le Domino Noir*.

Auer, Leopold (1845–1930), Hungarian violinist settled in Russia until the Revolution, when he went to the U.S.A. Pupil of Dont in Vienna and Joachim at Hanover, professor of the St Petersburg Conservatoire from 1868. Teacher of many eminent violinists.

Balakirev, Mily Alexeyevich (1836/7–1910), Russian nationalist composer, named by Glinka (q.v.) as his 'successor'. Self-taught, but a great inspirer of others. The most important members of his circle were Borodin, Cui, Mussorgsky and Rimsky-Korsakov (q.v.). Collectively they were known variously as 'the Balakirev circle', 'the Petersburg group', 'the new Russian school', and later as 'the mighty handful' (*moguchaya kuchka*), and in western Europe (but not in Russia) as 'the five'. Amongst his best works are a Symphony in C major; a piano concerto; a piano sonata; the Symphonic Poems *Tamara* and *In Bohemia*; and Incidental Music to Shakespeare's *King Lear*.

Belyaev, Mitrofan Petrovich (1836–1907), Russian timber merchant and keen musical amateur who sponsored symphony concerts and founded a publishing firm for the propagation of Russian music in 1885.

Bessel, Vassily Vassiliyevich (1843–1907), Russian music publisher, fellow-student of Tchaikovsky in St Petersburg, where he founded a publishing firm in 1869.

Boito, Arrigo (1842–1918), Italian poet, critic and composer, author of numerous libretti of Italian operas, including Verdi's *Otello* and *Falstaff*. Composer of the operas *Mefistofele* and *Nerone*.

Borodin, Alexander Porfirevich (1833–87), professor of chemistry and Russian nationalist composer, much influenced by Balakirev (q.v.) and one of 'the mighty handful'. Among his chief works are the opera *Prince Igor*, three symphonies (one unfinished) and a dozen masterly songs.

Brandukov, Anatol Andreyevich (1859–1930), celebrated cellist. Studied at the Moscow Conservatoire. Travelled much as a virtuoso.

Brodsky, Adolf (1851–1929), Russian violinist, pupil of Hellmesberger in Vienna; successively conductor at Kiev, professor at the Leipzig Conservatoire, leader of the Hallé Orchestra in Manchester and Principal of the Royal Manchester College of Music.

Bruch, Max (1838–1920), German composer, professor of composition in Berlin, 1892–1910.

Bülow, Hans von (1830–94), German pianist and conductor. His wife, Liszt's daughter Cosima, left him for Wagner.

Cui, César Antonovich (1835–1918), Russian composer, critic and authority on fortifications, of French descent and born in Poland. Studying military engineering in St Petersburg, he became intimate with Balakirev (q.v.) and was numbered among 'the mighty handful' chiefly because he supported its ideals by his writings, though his compositions in the early days were thought highly of by Balakirev.

Dargomyzhsky, Alexander Sergeyevich (1813–69), Russian composer who believed in 'truth' and 'realism' in music. He had no professional training, and some of his harmonic quirks which he would hardly have employed had he known the current harmonic 'rules' influenced later Russian composers, particularly Mussorgsky (q.v.). Besides his operas *Russalka* and *The Stone Guest*, his most important compositions are the Ukrainian 'Kazachok' for orchestra and some remarkable songs.

Fitzenhagen, W. K. F. (1848–90), German cellist, professor at the Moscow Conservatoire and a director of the Moscow branch of the Russian Musical Society.

Glazunov, Alexander Constantinovich (1865–1936), Russian composer, pupil of Rimsky-Korsakov (q.v.). His early musical nationalism gave way to eclectic tendencies; his large output includes eight symphonies.

Glinka, Michael Ivanovich (1803–57), Russian composer, often called the 'father' of Russian music. His only professional musical studies were with Dehn at Berlin in 1833. Most 19th-century Russian composers acknowledged their debt to him, and in the 20th century Stravinsky among others has done the same. Two of the most important facets of his influence are the nationalist tendencies in his two operas, *A Life for the Tsar* (1836) and *Russlan and Ludmilla* (1842), especially the latter, and the clear transparency of his instrumentation.

Hanslick, Eduard (1825–1904), music critic in Vienna, lecturer on musical history.

Hubert, Nicholas Albertovich (1840–88), son of a piano teacher and fellow-student with Tchaikovsky at the St Petersburg Conservatoire, became professor of theory at the Moscow Conservatoire and succeeded Nicholas Rubinstein as the Director of that institution.

Jurgenson, Peter Ivanovich (1836–1903), started a publishing house in Moscow in 1861 with the help of Nicholas Rubinstein, whom he assisted in the foundation of the Moscow Conservatoire. Besides publishing Russian editions of standard classics, he issued much music by contemporary Russian composers, including most of Tchaikovsky's.

Kashkin, Nicholas Dmitriyevich (1839–1920), Russian music critic and professor at the Moscow Conservatoire from its foundation in 1864 to 1896. Author of reminiscences of Tchaikovsky (see Appendix D).

Klindworth, Karl (1830–1916), German pianist and conductor, pupil of Liszt and arranger of vocal scores of Wagner's work. He had a school of music of his own in Berlin.

Kotek, Joseph Josephovich (1855–84), originally a pupil of Laub (q.v.) and Tchaikovsky, became resident violinist in Nadezhda von Meck's household.

Together with Nicholas Rubinstein he introduced his employer to Tchaikovsky's music. He was nicknamed 'Kotik' ('Tom-cat') by Tchaikovsky, and was responsible for his high spirits early in 1878 which led to the composition of the Violin Concerto, for which he gave valuable technical advice. Tchaikovsky visited him as he lay dying of tuberculosis in Switzerland in 1884.

Laroche, Herman Augustovich (1845–1904), Russian music critic, fellow-student of Tchaikovsky at the St Petersburg Conservatoire, professor at the Moscow Conservatoire from 1867. Returned to St Petersburg in 1871. Critic on many leading Russian newspapers.

Laub, Ferdinand (1832–75), Czech violinist, studied at the Prague Conservatoire, and in Vienna from 1847. Travelled much and succeeded Joachim as leader of the court orchestra at Weimar in 1853. He became principal violin professor at the Moscow Conservatoire in 1866.

Litolff, Henri Charles (1818–91), pianist, music publisher and composer of Alsatian descent. His overtures and works for piano and orchestra, now forgotten, were once popular, and his music was admired by both Balakirev and Tchaikovsky.

Meyerbeer, Giacomo (1791–1864), German-Jewish composer whose real name was Jacob Liebmann Beer. The huge success of his deliberately popular French operas, particularly *Robert le Diable, Les Huguenots* and *Le Prophète*, caused him to be reviled, envied and imitated in about equal proportions by other composers. His music was much more influential than is generally realized, but it is this aspect of it which is most interesting today and no revival of a Meyerbeer opera is liable to have much success, though certain individual numbers reveal his inherent musicianship and sense of tone colour.

Mussorgsky, Modest Petrovich (1839–81), Russian nationalist composer, pupil of Balakirev (q.v.) and one of the 'mighty handful'. Also much influenced by Dargomyzhsky (q.v.) and to a certain extent by Meyerbeer (q.v.). His finest works include the opera *Boris Godunov*, the original score of which is startlingly innovatory and reveals more deeply than any other work the true nature of the Russian national consciousness as displayed in the folk-idiom; the *Pictures from an Exhibition* for piano; and some strikingly original songs. With the possible exception of Borodin (q.v.), none of the other members of Balakirev's circle really understood the importance of these compositions. Tchaikovsky was similarly sceptical.

Nápravník, Eduard (1839–1915), born in Bohemia, studied at the organ school in Prague. Went to Russia in 1861 and became conductor of the St Petersburg opera, and of the Russian Music Society soon after Balakirev's resignation. He wrote four operas and numerous miscellaneous works.

Ostrovsky, Alexander Nicholayevich (1823–86), Russian dramatist, first practised as a lawyer and later became famous as author of many historical and sociological dramas.

Padilla y Ramos, Mariano (1824–1906), Spanish baritone singer, studied in Italy and toured Europe extensively. Married Désirée Artôt (q.v.) in 1869.

Petipa, Marius (1819–1910), dancer and choreographer, born at Marseille, made his debut at Rachel's benefit with Carlotta Gristi at the Comédie-Française. Went to St Petersburg in 1847 and became ballet-master at the Maryinsky Theatre.

Rimsky-Korsakov, Nicholas Andreyevich (1844–1908), Russian composer who began his career in the navy, but took to music after meeting Balakirev (q.v.), whose circle he joined. Became professor of composition at the St Petersburg Conservatoire in 1871. Like the other members of 'the mighty handful' his music grew steadily away from its earlier resemblance to Balakirev's. The transparency of his orchestration derives from Glinka (q.v.) and the cool, calm detached nature of his late music, together with its dry humour, influenced Stravinsky, who was his pupil. He wrote many operas of which the best known is *The Golden Cockerel*, and a number of brilliant orchestral works, as well as numerous miscellaneous compositions including some beautiful songs.

Rubinstein, Anton Grigorevich (1830–94), Russian pianist and composer, made public appearances from his ninth year and became one of the greatest pianists of his day. As a composer, though immensely prolific, he is now almost entirely forgotten. The *Ocean* Symphony and the opera *The Demon* were amongst his most successful works, and in spite of his initial eclecticism, he displayed nationalist tendencies in certain later works, particularly the Symphony in G minor. He founded the St Petersburg Conservatoire in 1862.

Rubinstein, Nicholas (1835–81), Russian pianist and conductor, brother of the preceding. Studied in Berlin, founded the Russian Musical Society at Moscow in 1859, and the Conservatoire there five years later.

Serov, Alexander Nicholayevich (1820–71), Russian composer and critic; studied law, but found time to cultivate music, which eventually, after a career as civil servant, he succeeded in taking up professionally. He greatly admired Wagner and propagated his music in Russia. His own operas *Judith* and *Rogneda* were enormously successful.

Siloti, Alexander (1863–1945) (otherwise 'Ziloti', according to the English transliteration), Russian pianist, student at the Moscow Conservatoire, 1875–81, and pupil of Liszt thereafter until the latter's death. Made extensive tours and became professor at the Moscow Conservatoire in 1890.

Smyth, Ethel Mary (1858–1944), English composer and author, studied at Leipzig, where she produced several works. Her compositions include the operas *The Wreckers* and *The Boatswain's Mate*, a cantata *The Prison*, etc.

Stassov, Vladimir Vassiliyevich (1824–1906), Russian critic and author, and champion of the nationalist school represented by 'the mighty handful', a term he himself coined in 1867. He had many ideas which he passed on to Balakirev, Mussorgsky, Borodin, Rimsky-Korsakov and Tchaikovsky about opera libretti, descriptive symphonic works or the use of folk-tunes. Balakirev's programme for Tchaikovsky's *Manfred* Symphony originated with Stassov, as did the programme for the symphonic Fantasia, *The Tempest*. After hearing Tchaikovsky's *Romeo and Juliet* Overture he remarked to Balakirev that 'the mighty handful' used to number five, but now it was six.

Taneyev, Sergei Ivanovich (1856–1915), Russian pianist and composer, student of Tchaikovsky at the Moscow Conservatoire, and succeeded his master there in 1878. His most important works, of a certain academic solidity, are orchestral and chamber music.

Viardot-Garcia, Pauline Michelle (1821–1910), Franco-Spanish soprano singer.

Zaremba, Nicholas Ivanovich (1821–79), professor of theory at St Petersburg Conservatoire from its foundation in 1862. Believed in the educational efficacy of Strict Counterpoint. Succeeded Anton Rubinstein as Director of the Conservatoire from 1867 to 1871. Is lampooned in Mussorgsky's song *The Peepshow*.

Zvantsev, Constantine Ivanovich (1823–90), music critic, eminent translator, librettist, contributor to the journal *Art*. Together with D. Lobanov and A. Maikov wrote the Russian version of the libretto of *Judith* by Serov (q.v.).

Appendix D

Select bibliography

IN RUSSIAN
A complete bibliography of Russian works on Tchaikovsky would require an entire volume. This select bibliography is restricted to the main sources used in the book. The reference letters are those quoted in the footnotes.

RA Balakirev, M. A., *Vospominaniya i Pisma* (Recollections and Letters), Leningrad, 1962. This volume includes 'Perepiska s P. I. Tchaikovskim' (Correspondence with P. I. Tchaikovsky) edited with notes by A. A. Orlova (pp. 115–203).

RB Kashkin, N. (1) *Vospominaniya o P. I. Tchaikovskom* (Recollections about P. I. Tchaikovsky), Moscow, 1896; supplemented by (2) 'Iz vospominany o P. I. Tchaikovskom' in *Proshloe Russkoy Muzyki*, Petrograd, 1920. (New edition, Moscow, 1954.)

RC Laroche, H., *Sobranie Muzykalno-kriticheskikh Statei* (Collection of articles of Music Criticism), 2 vols., Moscow 1922, 1924.

RD Rimsky-Korsakov, N.A., *Letopis moei Muzykalnoy Zhizni* (Chronicle of my Musical Life), St Petersburg, 1909.

RE Shaverdyan, A. I. (ed.), *Tchaikovsky i Teatr: Stati i Materialy* (Tchaikovsky and the Theatre: articles and materials), Moscow-Leningrad, 1940.

RF Taneyev, S.I., *P. I. Tchaikovsky; S.I. Taneyev; Pisma* (Letters), Moscow, 1951. This volume, edited by V. A. Zhdanov, includes the following:
(1) P. I. Tchaikovsky – S. I. Taneyev: Perepiska (Correspondence) (1874–1893), pp. 3–201.
(2) P. I. Tchaikovsky – A. P. Merkling (1871–1893), from p. 205.
(3) P. I. Tchaikovsky – N. G. Konradi (1876–1893), from p. 257.
(4) P. I. Tchaikovsky – Y. P. Shpazhinskaya (1885–1891), from p. 288.
(5) P. I. Tchaikovsky – N. A. Plesskaya (1879–1893), from p. 361.
(6) P. I. Tchaikovsky – Désirée Artôt (1888–1890), from p. 371.
It also includes correspondence between Taneyev and third parties.

RG Tchaikovsky, I.I., *Dnevniki P. I. Tchaikovskovo* (Diaries), Moscow-Petrograd, 1923.

RH Tchaikovsky, M.I., *Zhizn Petra Ilyicha Tchaikovskovo* (Life of Peter Ilyich Tchaikovsky), 3 vols., Moscow, 1900–2.

RI Tchaikovsky, P., *Literaturnye Proizvedeniya i Perepiska* (Literary Works and Correspondence). In this 'complete' collection, Tchaikovsky's letters start at Vol. V (Moscow, 1959) and finish at Vol. XVII (Moscow, 1981).

RJ Tchaikovsky, P.I., *Perepiska s P. I. Jurgensonom* (Correspondence with P. I. Jurgenson), edited by V. A. Zhdanov and N. T. Zhegin, 2 vols: Vol. I, Moscow, 1938; Vol. II, Moscow-Leningrad, 1952.

RK Tchaikovsky, P.I., *Perepiska s N. F. von Meck* (Correspondence with N. F.

von Meck) edited by V. A. Zhdanov and N. T. Zhegin, 3 vols., Moscow, 1934–6.

RL   Tchaikovsky, P. I., *Pisma k Blizkim: Izbrannoe* (Letters to Relations: Selection), edited by V. A. Zhdanov, Moscow, 1955. This is an expurgated version of 'Pisma k Rodnym', printed in 1940 but suppressed before publication.

RM   Tchaikovsky, *Tchaikovsky i Zarubezhnye Muzykanty: Izbrannye Pisma Inostrannykh Korrespondentov* (Tchaikovsky and Foreign Musicians: Selected Letters of Foreign Correspondents), Leningrad, 1970.

RN   Yakovlev, V (ed.), *Dni i Gody P. I. Tchaikovskovo: lepotis zhizni i tvorchestva* (Days and Years of P. I. Tchaikovsky: chronicle of his life and works) compiled by E. Zaidenshnur, V. Kiselev, A. Orlova and N. Shemanin, Moscow-Leningrad, 1940.

IN ENGLISH
Inaccurate and outdated books have been excluded.

EO   Abraham, Gerald. Important articles include the following:
From *Slavonic and Romantic Music*, London, 1968:
(1) 'Tchaikovsky: Some Centennial Reflections' (pp. 107–15), originally published in 1940.
(2) 'Tchaikovsky's Operas' (pp. 116–77), a revised and enlarged version of ER(7) below.
From *On Russian Music*, W. Reeves, London, 1939:
(3) 'The Programme of the *Pathétique* Symphony' (pp. 143–6).
(4) '*Eugene Onegin* and Tchaikovsky's Marriage' (pp. 225–33).
From *Studies in Russian Music*, W. Reeves, London, 1935 and 1969:
(5) 'Tchaikovsky Revalued'.

EP   Abraham, Gerald, *Tchaikovsky*, London, 1944.

EQ   Abraham, Gerald, and Lloyd-Jones, David, Authoritative Forewords to the following Eulenburg miniature scores: Symphonies Nos. 1 to 6 and *Manfred Symphony*; Piano concertos Nos. 1 and 2; Violin Concerto; Overture-Fantasy *Hamlet*; Symphonic Fantasia *Francesca da Rimini*; Suite from *The Sleeping Beauty*.

ER   Abraham, Gerald (ed.), *Tchaikovsky: a Symposium*, London, 1945.
This volume includes the following articles:
(1) Edward Lockspeiser: 'Tchaikovsky the Man' (from p. 9).
(2) Martin Cooper: 'The Symphonies' (from p. 24).
(3) Eric Blom: 'Works for Solo Instrument and Orchestra' (from p. 47).
(4) Ralph W. Wood: 'Miscellaneous Orchestral Works' (from p. 74).
(5) Colin Mason: 'The Chamber Music' (from p. 104).
(6) A. E. F. Dickinson: 'The Piano Music' (from p. 114).
(7) Gerald Abraham: 'Operas and Incidental Music' (from p. 124).
(8) Edwin Evans: 'The Ballets' (from p. 184).
(9) A. Alshvang (trans. I. Freiman): 'The Songs' (from p. 197).
(10) Gerald Abraham: 'Religious and Other Choral Music' (pp. 230–5).
There is also a good bibliography of volumes published before 1945.

ES   Evans, Edwin, *Tchaikovsky*, London, 1906, rev. 1935 and 1966.

ET   Friskin, James, 'The Text of Tchaikovsky's B♭ minor Concerto' in *Music and Letters*, Vol. 50, No. 2, pp. 246–51, London, 1969.

EU   Garden, Edward, *Balakirev: a Critical Study of his Life and Music*, London, 1967.

EV   Lakond, W. (ed.), *The Diaries of Tchaikovsky*, New York, 1945. This is an American translation of RG above.

EW   Tovey, Donald, *Essays in Musical Analysis*, 6 vols., O.U.P., London, 1935–9.
Included in the above are:
(1) 'Tchaikovsky: Symphony in E minor, No. 5, Op. 64', (Vol. VI, pp. 58–65).
(2) 'Tchaikovsky: Pathetic Symphony in B minor, No. 6, Op. 74', (Vol. II, pp. 84–9).

EX   Warrack, John, *Tchaikovsky: Symphonies and Concertos* (B.B.C. Music Guide), London, 1969.

EY   Weinstock, Herbert, *Tchaikovsky*, New York, 1943.

EZ   Westrup, J. A., 'Tchaikovsky and the Symphony', in the *Musical Times*, London, June, 1940.

An important reference book, which gives not only a comprehensive list of works but also quotations from contemporary documents etc., is:

Dombayev, G. *Tvorchestvo Petra Ilyicha Tchaikosvkovo* (The Works of Peter Ilyich Tchaikovsky), Moscow, 1958.

ADDENDUM

All four volumes of David Brown's definitive work, *Tchaikovsky: a biographical and critical study*, have now been published: Vol. I, *The Early Years, 1840–1874* (London, 1978); Vol. II, *The Crisis Years, 1874–1878* (London, 1982); Vol. III, *The Years of Wandering, 1878–1885* (London, 1986); Vol. IV, *The Final Years, 1885–1893* (London, 1991).

There are two important articles concerning Tchaikovsky's death:
Alexandra Orlova (trans. David Brown), 'Tchaikovsky: The Last Chapter' in *Music & Letters*, April 1981, Vol. 62, No. 1, pp. 125–45.
Alexander Poznansky (trans. Ralph C. Burr, Jr.), 'Tchaikovsky's Suicide: Myth and Reality' in *19th Century Music*, Spring 1988, Vol. II, No. 3, pp. 199–220.

Two books of translations into English by Galina von Meck of Tchaikovsky's correspondence are:
Edward Garden and Nigel Gotteri (ed.), with an Introduction by Edward Garden, *To my best friend: Correspondence between Tchaikovsky and Nadezhda von Meck, 1876–78* (Oxford, 1993). This is a translation of RK, Vol. 1.
Percy Young (ed.), *Piotr Ilyich Tchaikovsky. Letters to his Family: an autobiography* (London, 1981). This is a translation of RL.

Other recent books in English which are recommended for further reading:
Alexandra Orlova (trans. R. M. Davison, with a Foreword by David Brown), *Tchaikovsky: A Self-Portrait* (Oxford, 1990).
Alexander Poznansky, *Tchaikovsky: The Quest for the Inner Man* (New York, 1991).
R. J. Wiley, *Tchaikovsky's Ballets* (Oxford, 1985).
E. O. Yoffe, *Tchaikovsky in America: the Composer's Visit in 1891* (New York, 1986).
Henry Zajaczhowski, *Tchaikovsky's Musical Style* (Ann Arbor, 1987).

For a fuller select bibliography, see Vol. IV of David Brown's work (listed above), pp. 489–91. For a complete bibliography, see David Brown's 'Tchaikovsky' in *Russian Masters, 1* (London, 1986); this is a revised reprint of the entry in *The New Grove Dictionary of Music and Musicians* (London, 1980) with the bibliography updated to 1985.

Index